MOVING: *THE CHALLENGE OF CHANGE*

A GUIDE TO SUCCESSFUL
GEOGRAPHIC RELOCATION

MOVING

THE CHALLENGE OF CHANGE

MARGARET B. EMERSON
AND
CATHERINE CAMERON

ABINGDON PRESS • NASHVILLE

MOVING: The Challenge of Change

Copyright © 1988 by Abingdon Press

This book is printed on acid-free paper.

Library of Congress Cataloging-in-Publication Data

Emerson, Margaret, 1930–
    Moving: the challenge of change.

    Includes index.
    1. Moving, Household. I. Cameron, Catherine.
II. Title.
TX307.E454   1988   648.9   88-10564
ISBN 0-687-27261-0 *(alk. paper)*

MANUFACTURED BY THE PARTHENON PRESS AT
NASHVILLE, TENNESSEE, UNITED STATES OF AMERICA

To the many men and women and children
who took the time to share their experiences
of the
challenges, problems, and opportunities
of
geographic relocation
and to our husbands,
James Gordon Emerson
and
Stuart Oskamp,
who have supported us in this endeavor.

CONTENTS

INTRODUCTION

So you're thinking about moving, or perhaps you have recently moved. Yearly, forty million other Americans have the same idea. They stuff their cars, rented trucks, or giant vans with all their worldly possessions and set off for greener pastures.

Usually, relocation is voluntary and promises a higher standard of living. Yet psychologists, sociologists, and mental health professionals agree that moving is a time of stress and potential crisis. Almost every American has faced the experience at least once, but for some individuals and families, moving is a way of life and not necessarily one that they have mastered. Some of them relocate as often as our nomadic ancestors. A major difference is that those ancient wanderers didn't have to pack several tons of furnishings, and they took all the people they knew and cared about with them.

The experiences of moving can be rewarding, uneventful, or seriously upsetting. Sometimes a past move proves to have been a turning point in life: its impact lives on into the present and may affect the future as well.

Those who are disturbed by moving tend to think that their feelings are unique. They may even blame themselves for not coping better with such a common human experience. That is why we wrote *Moving: The Challenge of Change*. In this book, we explore the challenge of relocation from the point of view of its personal and social impact as well as from a practical standpoint. *It is a book for and about people who move.* From its pages sound the voices of many Americans. Their accounts of the disruption and readjustment of moving—its joys and disappointments, gains and losses—have helped make possible this guide to successful relocation.

Our goals foryou, our readers, are as follows: First, we want to affirm your experiences, emotions, and reactions. Second, we want to provide you with proven ways of coping and practical suggestions for relocation. Third, we want to challenge you to take charge of your move and to make it an opportunity for personal growth.

Before doing our survey for this book, we read scores of research studies on moving. These were found in scholarly journals that the average person doesn't have the occasion to read. We raided the ivory towers of learning for ideas that would help people understand the complexities of change, crisis, and coping as these apply to moving. In addition, over a two-year period we gathered practical and personal information through two basic survey methods—questionnaires and interviews. The interviews were both brief and in-depth.

In this exploratory study, over three hundred interviews and questionnaires were analyzed. The majority of those with whom we talked were middle-class persons from the western part of the United States, but breadth was added through contacts in other parts of the country. At conferences the topic of relocation was discussed, and many interesting experiences were shared by participants.

We asked the movers themselves what they saw as the important issues in the ambivalent experience of moving, why moves generate excitement and hope as well as create depression and anxiety. The formal sample (persons who received questionnaires or who were interviewed in depth) was largely purposive and voluntary. We sought out those who would represent dual career and homemaker-career couples, singles, corporate employees, military personnel, college students, divorced persons, retirees, and children. We wanted to document the variety of issues and patterns in the experience of moving, which we felt would be helpful to our readers.

Moving: The Challenge of Change is divided into three parts. Part I is entitled *Moving: What's It All About?* Chapter 1 discusses "The Meaning of a Home." It shows that across time and culture there are certain general concepts of "home" and, therefore, implications for the idea of moving. But special meanings arise for each of us around the homes we have known; these come from our unique combination of past experiences, present circumstances, and future hopes. We present a questionnaire that will elicit the feelings you have toward your present home. It can also help you get in touch with your emotional, as well as intellectual, responses.

Chapter 2 focuses on the process of "Deciding Whether to Move." What triggers the decision to move? Who makes the decision and why? Who benefits and who pays? What about the question of fairness to everyone concerned? Chapter 2 includes a questionnaire to help you with your decision and to provide practical suggestions for you and your family.

Part II is entitled *Who Are the Movers?* In consecutive chapters of this somewhat more objective section, we discuss the findings of our research and give some helpful suggestions from our interviewees. We explore "Couples Going Places," "Children and Moving," "Singles on the Move," and "Situational Moves" as described below.

What happens in dual career marriages when a move is decided upon? The careers of men still dictate most moves, but the influence of employed wives is increasing. In 10 percent of the situations, husbands are now moving for their wives' careers. In this chapter, we also explore commuter marriages and homemaker-career family moves. Multiple moves form another topic. Whether it's his move, her move, or their move, relocation is not as simple as it used to be.

The family is more than a single unit. It is a collection of individuals. Each member—depending on age, sex, and personal needs—experiences a move differently. Children, whose feelings are often overlooked, mourn the disruption of their schooling and friends. How can they be helped?

The singles' chapter includes moves to college, moves for jobs or relationships, and moves after a divorce. Each of these topics has a different thrust. Going off to college is not the same as seeking a first job. And what about divorce? What influences the choice of moving or staying at the time of such a traumatic experience?

The chapter on special situations turns to a variety of specific moves. Military duty moves, international moves, and moves at the time of retirement are all explored.

Part III is entitled *The Process of Moving: Practical and Psychological Issues.* In this section, we specifically focus on you, the reader, giving concrete suggestions that will help you put your best effort into making successful moves. Chapter 7 gives "Practical Tips for Moving." There are many pressures leading up to moving day. Preplanning gives purpose to a hectic day and confidence that order lies beyond the present chaos. Weary movers demolish a pizza amid unopened boxes and begin the settling in process. How can all this happen as smoothly as possible so that one can feel "at home" again?

Chapter 8 focuses on "Stress and Coping." Moving can be a crisis, precipitating both problems and new opportunities. It is typically more stressful psychologically than physically, and even the happiest relocation can put one's usual coping mechanisms on overload. This chapter suggests ways to make a satisfactory adjustment.

Finally, the epilogue reminds you that "It's *Your* Move." Now is the time to celebrate and begin the new adventure with an awareness that you have the power to move ahead. You can design your own move rather than just let it happen.

We are grateful to the many people who were willing to be a part of our study and thus to reach out to others through their experiences. This is *their* book as well as ours. As you interact with other people in reading it, it will be *yours* as well.

MARGARET EMERSON
CATHERINE CAMERON

PART I

Moving:
What's It All About?

CHAPTER 1

The Meaning of a Home

Mid pleasures and palaces though we may roam,
Be it ever so humble, there's no place like home.
"HOME SWEET HOME!"—JOHN H. PAYNE

American playwright John Howard Payne had high hopes for success when his opera *Clari, the Maid of Milan* opened, but it survived only a dozen performances. A song included in that opera, however, won him international fame. It was called "Home, Sweet Home!" More than 150 years after it was first sung, this song still strikes a responsive chord in the hearts of millions of people.

The reason for this response is that a home is not just a house. Home has special meanings far beyond the practical one of a shelter from danger, sun, and storm. In this first chapter, we will explore these meanings and the emotions that are aroused by a deep attachment to a home. Some of these meanings are universal and have transcended time and culture. Others are unique to the individual.

Universal Meanings

From the caves outside of Beijing, China, where prehistoric man lived, to the modern houses of today, one of the most important functions of a home has been as a physical, emotional, and spiritual retreat. To be without this protective sanctuary is the ultimate insecurity. This view is even written into the English language: the infinitive *to be*—symbol for existence itself—originally suggested "place-dwelling" or being at "home."[1]

Today, the high stress level at which most of us function makes our homes especially important havens of familiarity and security; we can escape outside pressures and reconnect with our deepest selves.

> Our cabin in the woods is a precious place to me. When I was a child my mother used to take me there when I felt "stressed out." Now, when I return, I feel a sense of comfort and of peace as soon as I walk through the door.

The home has also been a place for teaching basic religious beliefs. Prehistoric caves were decorated with semi-religious art, and the earliest homes built by human hands were often places of worship as well. This is also true in many Judeo-Christian homes today, in which religion is an integral part of family life. Church denominations have ceremonies for the blessing of a new home; Beethoven lent his genius to composing an overture for "Consecration of the House."

Home also represents your "self" in all its aspects—body, soul, and personality. Frequently children's drawings express this physical symbolism. A house easily conjures up the image of a face: windows are eyes (shutters or blinds can close off what goes on within); a door is the mouth; turrets are ears; and a gable is the nose.[2]

Spiritually, the New Testament calls our bodies "temples of the soul" and instructs us to care for them accordingly. A famous parable describes a man who neglected his home (or soul). He rid it of an evil spirit but forgot to fill its emptiness. A host of demons rushed into the vacuum and took over (see Luke 11:24-26). The sacred writings of other traditions also make a connection between home and soul. The Chinese words for the spirit's departure at death mean "breaking the roof."[3]

In the psychological dimension, dream analysts since Daldlianus in the second century A.D. have interpreted home and house as metaphors for the self. You will understand this relationship if you ever come home to find that thieves have broken in while you were away. This situation creates a tremendous sense of personal, even physical, violation. As one man expressed it, "I believe that I now have some idea of what rape must feel like."

Underscoring this connection, a woman remarked: "It is terribly important to me when I move into a new setting to achieve order as soon as possible. It has a dramatic impact on my self-confidence." In addition, feelings about the self influence our living situations. A perceptive man who lived alone observed:

> I haven't been feeling very good about myself recently. My house is a mess. There is no comfort there. It's as if the disorder reflects my sense of self—the state of my ego.

Therefore, your home environment not only *reflects* self image, but also profoundly *affects* it. For example, making a change in a demoralizing situation by moving from a place you intensely dislike may be a first step to changing your self-concept. Again, this underscores the many ways in which home is a symbol of personhood.

Just as home environment and self are linked, our natural environment is part of the significance home holds for us. In fact, easy access to nature is the most important predictor of satisfaction with a living situation.[4]

Contact with nature taps deep emotions and gives us a sense of stability and continuity. Anyone who has gone camping knows that people go to a lot of trouble—insects, bugs, inconveniences—to reconnect with nature and thus with themselves. We are fortunate indeed when natural resources are available close to home, especially when we feel most needy.

> We lived far away from my mother when she was dying, and the distance was hard to bear. There was a park not too far from our home to which I would go every day to walk alone. I felt such comfort and peace there. It made me feel closer to her.

The strong bond among environment, home, and self has been evidenced throughout history in the frequent use of local materials to build dwellings. Archeologists tell us that the womb-like huts in Paleolithic camps were constructed from the branches of local trees. The skin homes of the Eastern Gravatian culture reflect a plentiful assortment of animals. Their portability allowed the inhabitants to move on in search of game and vegetation in that barren land. Such dwellings were the mobile homes of that day.

Today, as in the past, sensitive architects and builders combine nature and need, integrating homes into the landscape and capturing the multiple textures, tones, and shapes of nature. Such homes appeal to us with their harmony of earth, tree, and sky. A recent newspaper article featured a home designed to blend into the country hillside. Corn, asparagus, and wildflowers were to be planted on the roof. How would you like to pick your dinner vegetables and flowers for the centerpiece without leaving your house?

The meanings of *home* that have been explored in the past few pages are relatively universal. They expand on the basic idea of home as a place of shelter and sanctuary.

Personal Meanings

Beyond these collective meanings that humanity has brought to its dwelling places over time and across culture, there are meanings about the concept of home that are unique to each one of us. A single man expressed his feelings:

> Home is one of the most intimate words in our vocabulary. . . . [It] is the place where we belong in this vast universe. . . . Most of us work hard in another place, usually for other people, paying scant attention to our own needs. At the end of the day we turn homeward, undressing mentally and emotionally on the way. The "uniforms," "jackets," and "overalls" of the job are unbuttoned. The tie may actually be slipped off in the car. We push open the door with a sigh of relief. If anyone is there we call out, "I'm home!" If we live alone we mutter, "Home! Finally!"[5]

The image of home is not an empty one. As we mature, we experience our living situations—important events, persons, and places—as present within us rather than as something inanimate and external. Can you separate out who you are from the friends and relatives who have influenced you or from the house and neighborhood that sheltered you in your growing years? What of the home where you started a family of your own? These homes are populated by the people with whom you have shared them—your family of origin or the family you created. We all recall interchanges with parents, siblings, and children.

John Bowlby is a psychiatrist who has studied our attachments to people, places, and things—and our reactions to their loss.[6] Positive or negative emotional bonds form between individuals and their home environments. Such bonds can generate feelings on a continuum from a mild to a powerful response depending on the quality of previous homes and how many, how important, and how deep the needs are that are met in the present home setting.[7]

If we return to a former home, we find it filled with ghosts and memories: Mother coming to greet us down the long hall; Father teaching a bedside prayer; parents angry about something we didn't understand; secrets shared with a sister; a brother returning home from the war; a dark and scary attic; joy in childhood games. The smell of warm cookies fills the air, and piano keys (quiet for so many years) sound once more in our memories.

Unfortunately, homes do not always come equipped with warm feelings. Some among us find that the words *home* and *family* conjure up a multitude of unhappy memories. The song "Home, Sweet Home!" mocks our hurt, when growing up was a lonely or even brutal experience or when a marriage, begun in joyful expectation, ends in bitterness. A seventeen-year-old college girl wrote, "I will never go home again." Her short comment summed up escape after years of abuse. A divorced man said, "Every part of our home and neighborhood reminds me of painful interactions with my ex-wife." Home holds bitter meanings for these lonely people; yet, their longing for the kind of home and family that "should have been" remains. It keeps them looking for what they lost or never had. It is hard to find any substitute for these basic gifts, which we believe are our human heritage.

All of our meanings—positive and negative, collective and personal—come together in powerful feelings. They help form our outlook on life in general and our concepts of *home* and *family* in particular. If we find or create a living situation that satisfies our most important needs in meaningful ways, we do not want to unsettle that delicate and hard won balance.

Moves, therefore, can disrupt our fundamental structure of meaning, and leaving a home to which we feel a powerful emotional attachment causes a deep sense of bereavement. Frequently neither those traumatized by a move nor their families and friends can understand how great this impact can be; something must be wrong with anyone who is so desolate from the loss of home and community. Few people realize that reactions to severe grief are similar in depth and intensity whether the loss involves a spouse, a limb, or a home.[8] Patience and understanding are needed during the mourning period.

Before we can begin shifting loyalties to a new home, however, we must understand our attachment to our current one. This can dissipate some of the pain of leaving, help us to look forward rather than backward, and clarify what will be important to us in a new location. It is easier for us to handle changes if we can anticipate them and begin ahead of time to shift our attachments. If a move is unexpected, new attachments must be found later.

> After we moved, I realized how important the Vermont mountains had been to me. They had given me a sense of stability and inner peace. I was able to substitute some hiking trails not far from my new home and recaptured my serenity.

If conflict or pain has been associated with a particular home, we may be eager to leave. A cartoon by James Thurber shows a mild looking man returning home; his overpowering wife and their house were drawn as one. It might be a great relief to leave a home with such ominous associations. When we have no positive attachments, people-place bonds can be easily broken. The heart and mind are ready for change.

There was little I liked about where we lived in northern Maine. The natural environment was beautiful, but I had no friends, and my husband was gone for days on special projects for the corporation. I was so lonely, I could hardly wait to leave.

The Affective Quality of Place

What about you? As you think about the possibility of moving, what feelings does your home evoke in you?

Russell and Pratt compiled a list of negatively and positively keyed adjectives to tap into these feelings.[9] We have put some of these together in a questionnaire with our description of how to score it. By answering this questionnaire, you can understand more clearly how you feel (as well as think) about your current living situation. (You may want to take it twice: once for your home and again for your community. The two scores may be quite different.)

Your Feeling Response to Your Home*

The following list of words can be used to describe places. Please rate your *agreement or disagreement* with how well these words describe your feelings about your *current home:*

5 = AGREE STRONGLY	2 = DISAGREE SLIGHTLY
4 = AGREE SOMEWHAT	1 = DISAGREE SOMEWHAT
3 = AGREE SLIGHTLY	0 = DISAGREE STRONGLY

* Copyright 1980 by the American Psychological Association. Adapted by permission of the publisher and author.

Please be sure to give a number for *TO EACH ITEM* below.

To me, my current home feels:

1. Arousing   —   6. Displeasing   —   11. Beautiful   —
2. Tense   —   7. Alive   —   12. Inactive   —
3. Serene   —   8. Frenzied   —   13. Pleasant   —
4. Dull   —   9. Stimulating   —   14. Slow   —
5. Interesting —   10. Uncomfortable—   15. Restful   —
                    16. Dreary —

ADD your scores for EVEN and ODD numbered items *separately.*

Total for *odd* numbers   ——— ———

Total for *even* numbers   ——— ———

Subtract for the difference   ——— ———

A score of +20 or above suggests strongly positive feelings toward your current home.

A score of -10 to +10 suggests indifferent feelings toward your home.

A score of -20 or below suggests strongly negative feelings toward your current home.

The positive or negative slant of your final score will help you to understand how strong your emotional attachment is to your present home or community. The depth of this attachment will affect your adjustment to a new place. The questionnaire also suggests important qualities to look for in a new home.

As you think about moving, it is helpful to realize that your first impression of any new home and environment will be an emotional one. This first impression can be prophetic, determining the direction of your later feelings.

When we checked out the possibility of moving to Denver, we rented a car and drove into the mountains. There were fields of cattle minutes from Denver. Having lived most of my life in New York City, I was astonished to see cattle grazing just outside the city limits. It reminded me of the Canadian countryside and of childhood summers on farms. In that instant my roots sank deep. I was ready to move.

A different first impression affected a single man: "New York City engulfed me with its hugeness when I arrived. The noise, the masses, the dirt were overwhelming. I felt an incredible sense of aloneness. Two years were all I could stand."

For both of these people, their primary emotional responses had a lasting effect and helped to determine their positive or negative attachments. If you realize how important your emotional reactions are to future satisfaction in a new location, you are likely to give them equal weight with the practical and rational aspects of a move. (If you have enough information for an honest appraisal, you may even want to retake the questionnaire for the home and environs you are considering.)

Considering the many collective and personal meanings that we bring to our homes and living environments, the nostalgia or antipathy evoked by "Home, Sweet Home!" is no surprise. Now that you have more understanding of what your current home means to you, we will turn to the chapter on making the decision whether or not to move.

Notes

1. Martin Heidegger, "Building, Dwelling, Thinking." In *Basic Writings* (San Francisco: Harper, 1977), p. 321.
2. Carl Jung, *Man and His Symbols* (New York: Doubleday, 1964), p. 78.
3. Oliver Marc, *Psychology of the House* (London: Thames and Hudson, 1977), p. 67.
4. Marc Fried, "Residential Attachment: Sources of Residential and Community Satisfaction." *Journal of Social Issues* 38, no.3 (1982):114.
5. Robert St. Clair, "I'll Be Going Home Tonight." Unpublished paper, San Francisco, September 1986.
6. John Bowlby, *Attachment and Loss*, 3 vol. (New York: Basic Books, 1969), vol. 1: *Attachment*, p. 309.

7. Sally Shumaker and Ralph Taylor, "Toward a Clarification of People-Place Relationships: A Model of Attachment to Place." In *Environmental Psychology: Directions and Perspectives,* eds. N. Feimer and S. Geller (New York: Praeger, 1983), p. 225.

8. C. Murray Parkes, "Components of a Reaction to the Loss of a Limb, Spouse, and Home." *Journal of Psychosomatic Research* 16, no. 5 (1972):347.

9. James Russell and Geraldine Pratt, "A Description of the Affective Quality Attributed to Environments." *Journal of Personality and Social Psychology* 38 (February 1980):311-22.

CHAPTER 2

Deciding Whether to Move

*I got off the plane in Seattle after visiting my parents.
My husband announced that we were going to move.
Three days later the house was sold. In a week we were
on I-5 heading south for an unknown destination.*

Few of us decide to move as impulsively or as unilaterally
as this couple, and few have no specific destination in mind.
In sharp contrast, a Vermont couple who wanted to live in
South Carolina watched and waited several years for the
opportunity that finally took them there. Both of these
examples are extremes, spontaneity versus lengthy preparation. Most Americans fall somewhere in between.

In this chapter, we will examine issues that affect the
decision of whether to move. We'll look first at the possible
trauma involved in relocation, second at why we move so
much despite this stress, and third at who influences the
decision. Fourth, we will turn to the rewards and costs of
relocation as these affect the choice of moving or staying.
Finally, you will have a chance to examine your own feelings
about your move with the help of a questionnaire.

Moving Can Be Hazardous to Your Health

Ambivalence can accompany the happiest relocation, and
stress begins with having to decide whether or not to go.[1]
Hives, ulcers, and nightmares may be evidence of this
pressure.

Part of the problem is that a decision seems so final. The

word *decide* means "to cut off" other choices, and that can be scary. Generally we take two or three months to make up our minds whether to go and another six months, or considerably longer, to adjust to the new location. During much of this time, we may feel as if we are on an emotional roller coaster.

Relocation is a strain in itself, but this is greatly increased by important losses—home, school, close friends and relatives, and familiar scenes and activities. Those who move experience many changes. Work situations, community atmosphere, life-style, and even climate and clothing may be different. Too often, a serious crisis erupts for one or more of those involved in the move.

Given these possible hazards, and the deep attachments to home that were explored in the first chapter, why don't we just stay put? What turns people into nomads, setting off for far horizons?

Why People Are on the Move

Usually decisions to relocate are work related. These moves may be voluntary or involuntary. Some people move to accept new jobs, and others must search for work because they have been laid off. Persons who are self-employed may choose to move, while employees are usually transferred by their companies. (Sometimes, an entire corporation relocates, taking along its staff.) Lately, there have been reminders of the Great Depression era; in spite of our general affluence, families are on the road because of unemployment in their hometowns and cities. In addition, many farm families, hard hit by economic change, have been forced to find new homes.

The desire to be closer to family is another major reason people decide to move. For example, a young couple may want their children to experience the love of grandparents. Similarly, retirees may move near their grown children in order to enjoy their enlarging families and to be near in case of illness. Moves that bring families closer reduce the chances of further relocation.

These two motives—work and family ties—are centuries old. The earliest nomads followed wild animal herds and gathered the fruits of the seasons as they traveled. With the establishment of villages, families chose to make their homes near kin.

A third motive for deciding to move has emerged only recently: the search for a better "quality of life." This is especially true among those who are educated, young, and in high status jobs. Their goal is to enjoy a richer life in every way—satisfying work, caring relationships, favorite leisure and cultural pursuits, and the opportunity for self-expression.[2] A better standard of living and a pleasant geographical environment are usually part of the package. The mountains, oceans, and warm weather draw families to the West and the South.

Single young people are among those seeking "quality of life." Trained for prime positions, they carefully select that part of the country in which they want to live and move to the chosen spot to launch their careers. Said one young man: "Even before my friends and I graduated from law school, we had decided we wanted to live in Los Angeles. We all got jobs in L.A. firms and crossed the country in a caravan of cars."

In contrast to these autonomous young people, the elderly may be moved against their wishes when they can no longer care for themselves. It is disorienting to be taken from familiar surroundings to a relative's home or to a nursing establishment. Retirees who have the money and wisdom to make decisions in advance can move into retirement communities of their choice, many of which provide guaranteed life care.

Other motives for moving could fill a book. A few examples will suggest the variety of reasons that send people packing.

Health is one factor. After Crystal Y. contracted emphysema, she moved to a dry, smog-free town in Arizona. The Butlers, whose son had asthma, moved to a dry part of Texas on the recommendation of their doctor.

Adventure is another motivator. Rachel B. interrupted a professional career when she **moved** to Boston for two years.

She wanted the excitement of a different setting, job, and friends, so she chose to do something a bit scary. Tom P., having no family ties, moved eight hundred miles to be part of the political campaign of a candidate he greatly admired.

Reputation may be a concern. Embarrassment in one community can trigger a move to escape problems or to gain a fresh start for facing them. After Phillip M. was forced into bankruptcy, he took his family to another state.

Some movers respond to **psychological needs.** Sally R. broke her parents' rigid control when she located a job several hundred miles away from them.

There are also **rolling stones**—repeaters when it comes to moving. Jack N. is a happy wanderer, enjoying a few months in one city before going on to the next one. Paul W. is career Army; his family has had two to three year stints in seven different places, courtesy of the government. His children have pen pals in three countries.

For some families, **personal and family growth** are the motives for moving. Elizabeth and Peter M. were concerned about the insularity of the town in which they lived. They were considering an overseas move so that their children could be exposed to other cultures and become bilingual. "Also, we see an opportunity to make a difference in the world."

Some move to **"find themselves."** Marleen W. put her belongings into storage and traveled the country for several months, searching for "the place where I belong." She eventually settled in a mountain community.

A **movie** motivated one couple. Jane and Ross P. were living in a distant city when they saw a movie featuring San Francisco. It reminded them of how much they had once loved that city, and they relocated within the year.

Necessity overcomes inertia. Mary and Peter Q's rented house was sold from under them. One bonus of their new home was a shortened commute. A twelve hour work day became a reasonable eight hours.

Undoubtedly you are familiar with other reasons for moves, and you may have other reasons yourself for considering a move. One study revealed that those who move for job related reasons tend to move to large cities, while those who move for other reasons—such as family concerns, quality of living, or a desire for rural values—seek out the smaller cities or towns.[3]

As we have just seen, many persons are relatively free to decide when and where they want to move. Other individuals, because of age, handicaps, poverty, or social change, have limited choices and, of course, varying degrees of willingness to move.

Families on the Move

When it comes to families, and there is freedom to make a choice, who makes that decision? To answer this question, we must first pose several others:

Who wants to move?
Who has the authority to decide?
How does personality influence decision making?

Let's look at these issues in turn.

Who Wants to Move?

Job related moves are usually initiated by people seeking new positions because they want more money, prestige, satisfaction and fulfillment, or because of a company transfer.[4] Those transferred have usually been men (approximately 92 percent, according to the Employee Relocation Council).[5] Most are family men. Recently, however, the situation has shifted. In 10 percent of the family moves husbands are moving for their wives' careers.[6]

Certainly, the moving industry has found regular customers in American businesses. Some big corporations are guided by the philosophy that frequent moves stimulate creativity in their employees and in the settings to which they are sent. Ambitious employees also believe that relocation is good for them. These wage earners are aware of the traditional management attitude of "those who put their career before anything else are the ones most likely to climb the corporate ladder quickly. Make no mistake about it!"[7] Such employees expect to move several times while with a company, and when the order comes, it usually signals a welcome advance in status and salary.

In the military, moves are even more mandatory; the decision is far removed from the family that is affected by it. Even professionals, such as lawyers, pastors, and college professors, find that relocation brings promotion faster than staying with the same institution.

Most corporations want rapid transition, and frequently employees are given a two- to four-week notice before they are expected to be on the new job. This usually means a prolonged separation (generally of at least eight weeks) before the family is reunited. It may be extremely hard on both those who move and those who stay behind. Many couples find this period the most disruptive part of the move and, in some marriages, a crisis point.

For example, one man beginning a new job indicated that hotel living and restaurant eating were very lonely. "My personal balance was all out of whack. I wasn't sleeping or eating well and had no one there with whom to discuss the stresses of the new job." Another man who moved for his wife found a six-week separation particularly difficult when he had the responsibility for packing and saying the final good-byes to family and friends. One of our respondents said, "Try your *best* to move together as a family."

As documented in the next chapter, recently there has been an increased resistance to moving, particularly in dual career marriages. Some wives are strongly opposed to relocating in general or to a particular move. For example, we talked to a young woman whose gentle manner covered intense pain. She had recently entered an exciting graduate counseling program and had found many empathetic friends among both professors and students. She kept quietly repeating, "I *don't* want to go. I *don't* want to go." But she went. Terminating her program in mid-semester, she packed the household belongings and joined her husband.

Other wives, however, may be just as eager as their

husbands to raise the family standard of living and are challenged by the idea of moving to another part of the country. One woman wrote: "I always enjoy moving. It is an adventure and a challenge. Even living six months apart was good for my relationship to my husband and my son."

Much depends on both the individual situation and one's attitude toward the move.

Who Has the Authority to Decide on Family Moves?

Persons who are single and unattached are reasonably free to decide on their own moves. However, what about moves that involve families? In the past, society has recognized several kinds of authority in the home: traditional, legitimate, and expert. Each has helped determine who should decide about relocating a family. We'll look first at how many men have held this authority in the past and then at how decision making is changing.

Traditional authority, over the centuries, has been assigned by custom and religion, and it almost always goes to men. With few exceptions, the eldest sons have inherited the family wealth, males have directed the destiny of clans, and husbands have determined where their families will live.

Women's attitudes are based on culture and are a powerful factor regarding perceptions of authority. According to two separate studies, approximately 80 percent of the women interviewed believed that women should be willing to move when their husbands have the opportunity for career advancement.[8] The wives blame themselves for their own sadness and fears, so they are apt to suffer in silence—and pay the price in depression and anger.

Even the relatives of reluctant movers are not likely to understand or sympathize. One wife said that her family would have been enraged if she had argued with her husband about moving. Another found her only consolation in her roles of supportive wife and "good sport." She could not have handled the guilt of refusing to move.

In most of the world's religions, men have had power over their families, and the belief has been reinforced that it is the wife's duty to submit to her husband's wishes (i.e., that it is up to the husband to decide upon a move, and the wife should go uncomplainingly along). Another way in which religion plays a role is in families where one or the other partner sincerely believes that it is God's will to move. God's will for our lives is difficult to discern and is hard for a spouse to question. One woman reported:

> I gave up when my husband said it was God's will that we move. There was no way to argue that point. I decided I had to change my attitude, although I had a nagging feeling that God was telling me *not* to move.

Legitimate power has been associated with the traditional roles of wage earner and homemaker—the "Job Boss" and "Kitchen Boss," as a perceptive child called her parents. Each role has separate areas of influence. However, if Dad is considered the head of household, he can act on behalf of the whole family. A decision to move everyone to another state, for example, can be seen as his to make.

Expert power implies special knowledge. People have generally assumed that the sole family wage earner knows best about decisions affecting his work. Few wives are in a position to question their husbands' knowledge about company transfers. For example, one woman's husband cautioned, "If I say no this time, there might not be another chance, or the next possibility could be much worse." He had heard alarming examples of crime ridden cities to which other employees had been sent. Indeed, there may have been a good deal of reality to his concerns.

Personality Styles as They Affect Decision Making

It may seem surprising that the personality styles of couples influence decision making, but they do. Carl Jung saw people as fitting into "psychological types," classified according to the way they approach life.[9] Two of his personality types—thinking-sensate and feeling-intuitive— are opposites and fit society's view of sex roles. Men are seen as "practical and logical," while women are viewed as "intuitive and emotional." We grow up conditioned toward living these stereotypes, which support the view that men are better suited to making decisions than are women. Jung, however, did not value one psychological type over another. Indeed, he stressed the need for balance. A logical approach and creative imagination can work together. Problems arise when either person sees his or her own view as "obviously" right and the other as wrong.

All of the above listed factors strengthen the belief in the husband's right to decide to move his family and in the wife's duty to follow. Is this situation changing? Many believe that it is. With younger couples in particular, when and whether the husbands relocate is becoming a joint decision. Also, in the eighties, the social status and influence of women continue to grow in both the home and the workplace. Positions in management, politics, and the professions are opening to them. In far more families than used to be true, women are making their own career decisions (including homemaking) and are being supported in these by their partners.

Counting the Costs and Rewards of Moving

Many people have told us about weighing arguments for and against a move. These respondents felt that it was important to be realistic about both the negative and the positive aspects of moving before making a decision. Most of their comments, as well as research on relocation, have focused on economic, social, and psychological losses and gains that may be experienced in a move. We'll share their views with you, and then you'll have a chance to clarify how you feel about your specific move.

Potential Costs in Moving

Economic Issues. Hidden financial costs are sometimes overlooked in moving. Relocation can be expensive. Look at some typical frustrations that one person experienced.

You fix up the old house so that it will sell and then buy another home in a more expensive area. This one needs refurbishing. The plumbing is bad, and the furniture doesn't fit. The movers charge a mint, and insurance can't make up for treasured items that are broken, scarred, or even lost. You are too tired from the move to want to fill out the insurance claims! The climate is different, so it's new clothes for one and all. And you don't know where to find dependable merchandise and services at reasonable prices.

No question about it, settling into a new community saps time, energy, and even resources.

Increased expenses may even be accompanied by decreased earning power. A major concern today is the loss of one spouse's employment. A promotion for the other partner with a sizeable gain in salary may not make up for it. This was rarely an issue even as recently as twenty years ago, since most wives did not work outside of the home, but today the salaries and satisfactions of both husband and wife need to be evaluated carefully before making a move. Otherwise there may be some unhappy surprises, as one man learned.

We had wonderful plans for what we were going to do in the Bay Area. We both love opera, symphony, and the theater. What better place to come for those kinds of experiences? Unfortunately, we forgot that they all cost money! Although I received a good raise, the loss of my wife's salary and increased expenses prevented our doing some of the very things that we'd moved for.

One respondent strongly suggested that some savings be set aside in order to keep up both the morale and the standard of living of the family while the unemployed spouse is looking for a job.

Social Issues. All of the women and many of the men to whom we talked emphasized the painful loss of friends, which is distressing enough in itself and is aggravated when there are barriers to making new ones. One woman indicated that pregnancy kept her housebound so that it was hard to meet people. Another said, "Don't move north in the middle of the winter. Constant snowstorms kept me from meeting even my neighbors."

Another kind of a barrier was discovered by one woman. She wasn't used to playing politics, but found that there was a powerful "pecking order" in her new community. The key was who invited you to dinner and who accepted your invitation.

Couples also mentioned major embarrassments that grew out of minor ignorances. These make them feel somewhat anxious when the possibility of another move comes up. "You learn local customs the hard way," a man reported. They moved north from a southern community and he and his wife found that bringing their three children to a dinner party was not the thing to do there. Some of their experiences later became family jokes, but not at the time.

It is important to recognize that different communities have different social rules. Try to find these out early. You can preface your question with the phrase, "Since I'm new to this area, could you tell me _____?" Social slips are understandable, but you don't want to arrive at 7:00 for dinner and find your hostess in the shower—as happened to one couple.

Saying hello and learning new rules is just as difficult for children and teenagers as it is for adults. A little girl shook hands and curtsied to her new teacher; that was expected at her East Coast school, but ridiculed in the West. One woman remembered herself at seven years old, wishing on a star. "I didn't tell my wish because I wanted so much for it to come true. I asked that the children in the city where we were going would like me."

Psychological Issues. Men and women who choose to relocate for career advancement—or whose employers send them elsewhere with a sizeable promotion—gain the stimulus, prestige, and salary of a new position. The work may be demanding, but they usually enter an environment that is structured to help them succeed. However, along with the enthusiasm they may have a considerable amount of anxiety about succeeding on the new job.

In addition, when starting a new position, as much as 22

percent of the employee's time may be spent adjusting to the new situation.[10] Said one interviewee, "Everyone knows that when you change jobs your focus and energy have to be totally involved in the new position in order to succeed." This means that he or she has very little left over to invest in the family and friends, either giving to them or receiving from them. This can increase the experience of loneliness and isolation.

After the "honeymoon" is over, there can be a letdown and a serious questioning of the decision to move. Perhaps the support staff is smaller than one was led to believe, or assumptions with regard to the design of the job are false. One man indicated that after a few months he found himself under the exact same pressures to perform from which he thought he had escaped. This is the experience of many.

To complicate the situation, spouses who follow often direct resentment at the person who most wanted the move. It is especially hard if the partner starts to verbalize reservations about the wisdom of the move. The feeling expressed can be, "You wanted it. Now stop complaining!"

Resentment can go in both directions. For example, the primary wage earner in a growing family may have moved, in part, to cover escalating family expenses or because the school system was inadequate in a particular location. For his or her family to complain bitterly can create considerable dissension.

Another potential liability is that a move can revive earlier separation trauma, along with distressing memories of divorce or bereavement. Issues that have been rumbling below the surface are brought to consciousness. Even feelings from childhood and infancy can be triggered. One woman wrote, "Relocation away from my family of origin brought up very painful, unconscious material from childhood." Some people are unable to adjust to a move successfully without reworking the original loss through counseling. To ignore the grief and plunge into the new life by covering up pain only superimposes a new loss on the earlier one.[11]

It is important to be aware of these potential problems so

that there is some understanding of the psychological costs that may be experienced. Awareness prepares you for dealing with what comes.

Potential Rewards in Moving

If the problems listed above were the only side of the coin, it is unlikely anyone would move regardless of motivation. However, our respondents were frequently enthusiastic about a variety of benefits that they had received. Their later decisions about relocating were often influenced by these positive experiences. They felt optimistic.

Economic Issues. A move is frequently accompanied by a raise in salary, which increases the standard of living. An unemployed wife may take this opportunity to get a part-time job, to launch a career, or to embark on earning a college degree.

> I had read in the *Times* of a pilot project in Westchester County that was offering a part-time Masters degree in my field of interest. I was delighted when we moved there, and I was accepted into the program. It was my debut into the world.

Even though there may be a loss of income, an opportunity for a different career decision may still be possible.

> I was close enough to retirement that I decided not to work again. For years I had worked two jobs, and I was really tired. I didn't want to have to start all over. I decided to do what *I* wanted to do.

Psychological Issues. Two potential gains of moving are family closeness and personal growth. We found a number of people who had moved locally, but had never left the city where they were born. A young couple explained that moving away from family and longtime friends resulted in marital closeness: "I think we *had* to get away in order to grow. We learned a lot about each other and about turning strangers into friends in a new neighborhood."

Some respondents spoke of the fact that going through the

struggle and the adjustment to a move also increased personal awareness and resulted in making some positive changes internally.

Social Issues. Many people we interviewed had learned new communication skills through meeting persons of various life-styles and different cultures. They became more adaptable and more willing to risk social, leisure, and work encounters. Others were aware that they had developed a deeper concern for newcomers. A New Jersey woman had a new understanding of people who move into big apartment complexes.

> I'll never look at a new neighbor in the same way again. I find myself making brownies and even a meal to welcome newcomers. Now I know how important it is to feel welcome, and it's a great way to get to know new neighbors and potential friends.

Adventure. There can be a sense of excitement about a move.

> We moved from the Midwest to New York City. The ethnic mix was fascinating. Taking the bus downtown was a stimulating experience. It was also good for the children to be exposed to totally different groups of people from those they were used to.

People talked to us about discovering other kinds of experiences. A couple from the Iowa plains took up backpacking in the Shenandoahs after moving to Virginia. A Mississippi family learned to ice-skate in Vermont. A man from Michigan came to love the shifting colors of the Arizona desert.

New Beginnings. Individuals are seldom totally content with their current situations. We talked to a number of people who translated relocation into new beginnings. A single woman, concerned about her drinking problem, decided that a move could help her break old patterns. She joined Alcoholics Anonymous, which also provided her with a warm support system in her new location. A man who had gone through a marital separation from his wife and an emotional breakdown, saw the move as a chance to start over in a new location "where nobody would know." A teenager, meeting an entirely new set of peers, changed his nickname from "Tubby" to "Tab." Working wives, restless in their current jobs but kept by inertia from making a change, worked part-time for a while or found challenging positions that affirmed their confidence. "I hadn't realized that I had so much to offer," said one of them. In all of these situations, making a choice to do something different was important.

Other Positive Factors. When a young man began to recognize the benefits of a planned move, the decision to relocate was easy.

> I didn't want to go at first, but I began to see some very real advantages. My wife and I were working split shifts in Chicago. The move would give us the chance to spend more time together. I particularly liked the idea of being close to both the mountains and the ocean.

Other positives mentioned were

Starting over with a new partner (after a divorce), developing mutual goals and mutual friends.
The chance to begin a family. Since I had to leave my job, the timing was right.
My wife and I changed our values by slowing down the pace of life. No more "keeping up with the Joneses."
New furnishings and carpets. It was like spring cleaning. We had the chance to decorate our home together.
Better health; my wife's asthma cleared up, and my stomach disorders (caused by stress on the job) went away.
Giving up a long distance commute. My husband commuted two thousand miles every weekend for three years. The commute became intolerable for all of us. We moved in order to be a family.
Improved marital relationship. We are much happier

since our move because we have shared many thoughts and feelings about this change.

As you've heard in these pages what other people have said, ideas of your own will have surfaced. All the potential advantages of a move deserve to be weighed against possible disadvantages before you make a decision. Now, if you want to determine what a particular move would mean to you, try the questionnaire that we've provided below. It may be used as we present it or modified to suit yourself.

Let's Look at Your Choices

It's easy to focus attention on the decision to move. Yet, deciding to stay where you are is not just a default position, but a legitimate choice in its own right. Remember also that to go or not to go are not the only options. Recently to wait has become an attractive choice. The decision can be to move, but not until a later, better alternative comes along or, perhaps, until a better time.

One couple who chose to wait because the time was wrong were delighted when the corporation for which one of them worked made the same offer to relocate three years later. Then the move was an opportunity instead of a problem and they left with a positive attitude. Many other choices for couples are discussed in the next chapter, and there are a multitude of issues to consider for each of these varied options. How can one come to a wise decision?

The philosophy and language of the marketplace can help. Any choice you make involves both gain and loss, and decisions hinge on the net difference between them. Whether you buy a car or sunglasses, you compare two or three alternatives in terms of the features that are important to you. You measure the rewards against the costs.

The dilemma in any decision is that you must give up the alternative choice. You can't remain where you are and move away at the same time. "I wish I could clone myself to be in two places at once." The alternatives, values, rewards, and costs of moving are presented for your consideration in the questionnaire below.

Using the Questionnaire

The questionnaire that follows allows you to examine your own expectations and to compare them with those of other family members. It has been used by singles, couples, and even by entire families. If you are single, you may have only yourself to consider in the decision as to whether or not to move. It's important to compare your options and to identify the issues that matter most to you. Families can do the same; however, family members should also compare their individual responses with one another.

The questionnaire clarifies what each person expects, realistically or not, from the move. A person's fantasies of a new situation may be quite different from objective reality. Sometimes these *expectations* can become a kind of self-fulfilling prophecy. When a single woman in middle management was transferred to another city, she believed that it would be hard to develop friendships. For a while that expectation created the barrier she had feared. On the other hand, overly high expectations—for example, making it to the top on the new job in a short time—bring disappointment.

The questionnaire also asks you the *significance* of items for you, making the scores more meaningful. If weather is not important to your children, the rainy climate of the new location won't bother them. However, if gray days make you depressed and irritable, the questionnaire will highlight a problem that could have a ripple effect through the family.

All in the Family. Although husbands are usually the initiators of a move, all family members are affected by relocation, and they want their feelings heard and respected before the decision is made. Joint consultation of husband and wife is not only reasonable, but it also carries a special bonus. Women who have played an important part in the decision making process before a move adjust better after it, as do other members of the family. Also, for the wife to be a part of the decision is crucial to a satisfying adjustment for the rest of the family, since the adaptation of the wife to a new home is a major factor in the adjustment of the rest of the family.[12]

Kids Can Help. Teenagers and younger children should be included for a full understanding of family attitudes. (Questions can be modified to suit their ages.) It's amazing how even a toddler's wishes can be learned by simply talking to the child. A single parent reported:

> My boy wasn't yet three when we moved in with a friend to save money. It was an immediate disaster, and my son and I were really upset. I found two studio apartments available on short notice and asked my son which he liked best. One was in our old complex, and he chose it. He was so right! The familiarity comforted both of us, and all our stuff fitted right in place.

Questions about whether, when, and where to move are not usually decided by children, but getting their viewpoint is important. Even if the final vote goes against the children, they know that they have been heard and that their parents will do their best to help them benefit from the decision.

What About Fairness? With the questionnaire, you can also assess whether family members expect the move to improve their own lives and in what areas. Comparing family scores alerts you to fairness issues—the possibility of one person getting all the benefits of relocation while another is miserable. A twenty-four-year-old woman said:

> We were sitting there, weighing the pros and cons, and all the cons seemed to fall on me. He'd have a new job. He'd be meeting new people right away. I felt I was being ripped away from my cozy environment, and I couldn't see beyond what there might be for me to gain. It turned out a lot better than I expected. Just having him happier at work has enhanced our home life greatly.

Problems around special needs and concerns become obvious. Will Dad's job satisfaction compensate for less time with the family? Will Mother be able to transfer her graduate study credits to another university? Will living near the beach comfort a shy boy who has lost his only chum?

Now you are ready to take the questionnaire. Make several copies before you start. Couples and family members should fill them out separately and then compare results.

INSTRUCTIONS FOR USING THE QUESTIONNAIRE

"TO MOVE OR *NOT* TO MOVE"

WEIGHING THE ALTERNATIVES

Give your own personal views.
There are no right or wrong answers.

Column 1: As you think about *what you value in life*

How important to you right now are the items on page 45?
In Column 1, write a number (0 to 4) opposite each item.

> 4 = most important
>
> 3 = important
>
> 2 = somewhat important
>
> 1 = slightly important
>
> 0 = irrelevant or unimportant

Column 2: As you think about *moving*

How rewarding or costly would each item be to you?
Write the number (+/-) that best expresses your feelings in Column 2

> +3 = Extremely *rewarding*   - 3 = Extremely *costly*
>
> +2 = Somewhat *rewarding*   - 2 = Somewhat *costly*
>
> +1 = Slightly *rewarding*   - 1 = Slightly *costly*
>
>   0 = neither rewarding nor costly

Column 3: As you think about *staying where you are*

How *rewarding* or *costly* would each item be to you?
Write the number (+/-) that best expresses your feelings in
Column 3

+3 = Extremely *rewarding*   - 3 = Extremely *costly*
+2 = Somewhat *rewarding*   - 2 = Somewhat *costly*
+1 = Slightly *rewarding*   - 1 = Slightly *costly*
            0 = neither rewarding nor costly

Column 4: Multiplying to find your item scores—*for moving,*

Item by item, multiply the numbers in Columns 1 and 2.
Enter totals in column 4 as your item scores for *moving.*
(You may get scores that are +, -, or 0.)

Column 5: Multiplying to find your item scores—*for staying,*

Item by item, multiply the numbers in Columns 1 and 3.
Enter totals in column 5 as your item scores for *staying*
(You may get scores that read +, -, or 0.)

for your total scores for the two alternatives, *moving* and
staying, add up column 4 and then column 5

Your Own Preferences About Moving

After all those concerned have taken the questionnaire,
they need to clarify their own feelings about what moving
will mean to them personally. This is done before any mutual
exchange of ideas.

Take a look now at your *summary scores* for (1) moving and
for (2) staying where you are. Later you can examine your top
priority items. You might find that 4 is not a high enough
value to put on an item that is crucial to you. Feel free to
increase the number value up to 8.

A Strong Preference

If one of your summary scores is highly positive and the
other is highly negative, then you obviously have a strong

preference for or against this move. Don't be surprised if your score is higher for staying than for leaving. The familiar is often more comfortable than the unfamiliar. Those who score high for moving generally don't have a strong attachment to their present location for any of a number of reasons. For example, a woman who had no problem agreeing to a move said, "We left the tension, stress, congestion, and the sometimes vindictive atmosphere of our former city."

If you do feel strongly one way or the other, how will you handle it if your spouse and children feel differently?

\# Are you willing to stand up for your own wishes?
\# Are you willing to accept a decision contrary to your own wishes?
\# Can you negotiate ways to make the move less threatening for those who are opposed to the move?

No Real Preference

Perhaps the choice between alternatives is not all that clear. If the summary scores are highly positive for both alternatives, you expect to be happy whether you stay or go. Congratulate yourself on your flexibility and positive outlook. In this case, you might decide to give your vote to your spouse, the kids, or the family dog.

If your summary scores are neutral or highly negative for both alternatives, you won't work up any enthusiasm whatever the decision. Packing up the household would seem like a lot of work for nothing, so your best choice would be to improve your current situation and wait for a more promising opportunity. However, if you are married and other family members really want to go, you might consider letting their eagerness carry you along. (You might also do well to take a look within yourself in case there is some neglected source of unhappiness in your life.)

Weighing Family Outcomes for the Good of All

For those who see equity (or fairness) as a primary value in relationships, no decision should be a win/lose situation

QUESTIONNAIRE: WEIGHING ALTERNATIVE CHOICES

Columns:	1 Importance of Each Item	2 Reward/ Cost of Moving	3 Reward/ Cost of Staying	4 Scores Cost of Moving	5 Scores Cost of Staying
ITEMS ARE BELOW:					
ROLE CHOICE:					
job/career/home/ volunteer/study	———X	———	———	———	———
STANDARD OF LIVING:	———X	———	———		
RELATIONSHIPS:					
with your spouse	———X	———	———	———	———
with your children	———X	———	———	———	———
with relatives	———X	———	———	———	———
with friends	———X	———	———	———	———
OTHER ATTRACTIONS:					
Home	———X	———	———	———	———
Community	———X	———	———	———	———
Health	———X	———	———	———	———
Weather	———X	———	———	———	———

OPPORTUNITIES:
Social ——————X—————— —————— ——————
Religious ——————X—————— —————— ——————
Cultural ——————X—————— —————— ——————
Recreational ——————X—————— —————— ——————
Personal Growth ——————X—————— —————— ——————

SELF-IMAGE:
As a partner ——————X—————— —————— ——————
As a parent ——————X—————— —————— ——————
Work/school/ ——————X—————— —————— ——————
Volunteering ——————X—————— —————— ——————
Overall self-image ——————X—————— —————— ——————
Respect of others for me ——————X—————— —————— ——————

OTHER FACTORS:
(specify) ——————X—————— ——————
——————X—————— ——————

TOTALS: SUMMARY SCORES FOR COLUMNS 4 AND 5

THE *INTERPRETATION* OF THE RESULTS FOLLOWS THE QUESTIONNAIRE where one must always sacrifice so that another will gain. Winning for everyone begins with a comparison of each person's separate expectations, overall feelings and preferences, and those special joys and hurts that are unique to each individual.

It's rare to find a family in which everyone enthusiastically agrees. A more likely outcome is that there will be a variety of opinions for a multitude of reasons. Working together to list reasons for and against each alternative pins down expectations and how realistic they are. It's helpful to get as much information as possible about the new situation. Telephoning the chamber of commerce, the newspapers, the churches, and the schools in the new place can fill your mail box (and your heads) with ideas that will put a possible move into a sharper focus. Your community library has information about the geography, industry, weather, and leisure pursuits of other areas of the country. If a corporation is pushing the move, it should provide you with contacts and information about the new community. Since you work for the company, make it work for you, also.

A family visit to the prospective locality may be well worth the time, effort, and cost involved. It could make family opinion shift toward greater agreement, or it might expose a deep rift that must not be ignored.

Sorting out what is most important to each family member and where each person's unique fears lie is usually helpful. For example, an athletic teenager may think that she won't find a girls' soccer team at the new school. A smaller child might get the idea that his dog can't go with him. These concerns can often be quickly settled.

Eventually, despite ambivalence, a decision is made. Sometimes you're surprised at how it turns out, as was the man who said:

> I had always thought of "moving up" in a career as "moving on," so I was alert to advances that would take us elsewhere. After careful investigation of two good offers in succession, my wife and I realized how much we enjoyed our current

work, our community, and our friends. We're now putting down roots with a far deeper appreciation of how really fortunate we are.

If a decision is made to move, many more contingent decisions follow. Where shall we live? Shall we rent or buy? (Some who have owned their homes find renting difficult because tenants usually can't decorate to their hearts' content, but others think it is the only way to go.) How long a commute would be acceptable and realistic? (Remember that the hours you are on the road are stolen from family time.) Is a reverse commute, against the traffic, an option? Will you live in a house or an apartment? A modern house or a traditional, older home? In the city or the suburbs? Be sure to check the noise level of the community before signing the contract. One of our respondents rented a house on a quiet day only to discover that the new home was in the flight pattern of an airport and that a barking dog across the street was never quiet. Another wrote:

> Don't try to duplicate the previous home, but enjoy the uniqueness of the new home and environs. We tried to superimpose one city on top of the other and made a bad and expensive choice. We should have rented for a while, gotten to understand what the new community had to offer, and then decided what to do.

Many other questions follow the decision to move. They can be used to negotiate issues with a reluctant mover, thus making leaving less painful.

Occasionally a couple or a family decides that a move is wise, or even unavoidable, in spite of someone's deep misgivings. Imbalance can cause resentment on one side and guilt on the other. It is essential, therefore, to give caring thought to improving the expectations of the reluctant mover.

1. *Start by identifying which aspects of the move are most threatening and which suggest at least some rewards.* One man reported that giving up his job to follow his wife to a teaching position was frightening. However, he decided that the

opportunity to freelance could open new avenues and offer freedom from what had become a rather routine job. Also, being supportive of his wife's getting her "dream job" increased his good feelings about himself in the marital relationship.

2. *Work out, with the family members, specific plans to minimize problems and to expand areas of possible satisfaction.* A twelve-year-old boy was devastated by a planned move from Pennsylvania to Long Island. Through visits to the new location he discovered that the town offered sailing lessons, which would allow him to make new friends while engaging in an exciting sport. His parents saw that he was immediately enrolled in the class.

3. *Consider these plans as a commitment to the reluctant mover and start implementing them as soon as possible.* If the troubled person happens to be you, don't be a silent martyr. Define your needs and wishes as clearly as possible. If you know what you want, you can set about achieving the goals. If relocation is inevitable, speak up about ways others can help to make it a brighter prospect for you, and be especially good to yourself at this time. Whichever way a difficult decision goes, a natural optimism gradually tends to take over. We begin to feel convinced that the choice we made was the right one, and thoughts about the abandoned choices trouble us less.

In Part III we will be exploring moves for different groups of people: couples, children, singles. We also include a chapter on military, international, and retirement moves.

Notes

1. Catalyst, *Human Factors in Relocation: Corporate and Employee Points of View.* A research project conducted by Catalyst, funded by Bekins Van Lines, 1983, p. 36.

2. Sally Ann Shumaker and Daniel Stokols, "Residential Mobility as a Social Issue and Research Topic." *Journal of Social Issues* 38, no. 3 (1982): 8.

3. James Christenson, Lorraine Garkovich, and Gregory Taylor, "Pro-ruralism Values and Migration Behavior." *Population and Environment* 6 (Fall 1983).172.

4. Larry Long and Kristin Hansen, "America on Wheels." *Society* 17 (March-April 1980): 77.

5. Catalyst, *Human Factors*, p. 2.

6. Carole Gould, "A Helping Hand for the 'Trailing Spouse.' " *New York Times* (February 22, 1987):11.

7. Alan Cox, "The Married Executive Has the Edge." *Across the Board* 20 (January 1983):25.

8. Jeanne Brett, "The Effect of Job Transfer on Employees and Their Families." In *Current Concerns in Occupational Stress,* eds. Cary Cooper and Roy Payne (New York: John Wiley and Sons, 1980), p. 112.

9. Carl G. Jung, *The Collected Works of C. G. Jung,* ed. William McGuire, vol. 6: *Psychological Types* (Princeton: Princeton University Press, 1959).

10. Mitchell W. Fields and James B. Shaw, "Transfers Without Trauma." *Personnel Journal* 64 (May 1985):60.

11. Thomas Holmes and Richard Rahe, " ['Misplaced Persons': The Crisis of Emotional Separation in Geographical Mobility and Uprootedness." *Journal of Psychoanalytic Anthropology* 7 (Summer 1984):278.

12. Stella Jones, "Geographic Mobility as Seen by the Wife and Mother." *Journal of Marriage and the Family* 35 (May 1973):211 and 213.

PART II

Who Are the Movers?
The People We Interviewed
and Their Experiences

CHAPTER 3

Couples Going Places

"Moving gradually creates lasting changes in almost every part of a couple's life." Many couples who have gone through long-distance moves would agree with that statement. However, the eventual outcome of relocation can be positive, despite the inevitable disruptions at first.

This chapter focuses on two basic kinds of couple moves: (1) moves for working couples; both partners are employed in jobs or careers, and (2) moves for traditional homemaker-career families; only the husband is employed. In most cases, the move is intended to benefit the whole family, even though a move is usually made to advance the husband's career. Each situation has special problems and opportunities.

The American family system has changed markedly in the last two decades. In 1985, half of the women with children under six years of age worked outside the home. This rate is almost double that of 1960. In 1983, two-thirds of the wives with grade school children worked outside the home.[1] Today, the traditional homemaker-career family is in the minority. The vast majority are dual-career families, worker-career families, and single-parent families.

Working Couples

In the worker-career family, both partners work, but they concentrate on the development of the one partner's profession. The purpose of the second job is for additional income (and perhaps personal satisfaction). In the dual-career family, both partners follow their own careers, which can be defined as jobs that are personally meaningful, that grow with one's abilities, and that demand strong commitment.[2] In addition, the partners actively support each other's career development and share the duties of family life.[3] Under these circumstances, the wife may earn as much or more than her husband.

Relocation affects couples in both of these life patterns. Surprisingly, however, couples seldom discuss their feelings or think through a general plan around moving in advance of a specific opportunity. Approximately two out of three corporate moves involve two-worker marriages.[4] Since this figure is going up rapidly, a couple invites crisis by delaying discussion until a move is in the offing. Emotions are apt to take over and rational thinking disappear. It is important to discuss the subject ahead of time and to have some kind of broad agreement. Discussion reduces unwelcome surprises.

In the past, a wife's work was rarely a relocation problem. As recently as twenty years ago, family roles were wage-earner, homemaker, and dependent children. Today, when the working wife moves for her husband (the typical case), she may suffer both economic and psychological losses, which are closely intertwined. Along with her job, she loses earning power and status in society. She finds herself in an unfamiliar dependent position. A move can send her from high to low status in the time it takes to pack a house. Even if her work was part-time, she discovers with dismay how important it has been to her sense of identity.

Finding a sympathetic ear to listen to her adjustment problems may be difficult. She is afraid of antagonizing new acquaintances who don't want to hear that she is unhappy in their community, and her busy husband may be desperately trying to keep his head above water on the new job. Her old support group is many miles away. She begins to wonder, "What's wrong with me, that I am so depressed?"

In addition, jealousy also enters, since her husband's earnings and status increase while hers decrease. "I became resentful that my husband always had a new and more important job to go to and a ready-made support structure. I was left to founder until I found a new job."

This is one reason why it is so important that the satisfactions of both the husband and the wife be evaluated in a move—as is suggested in the previous chapter. Also, considering our mobility, it is useful for men and women to try to build some flexibility into chosen careers. As one respondent said, "Many careers, with imagination, can be expanded into different kinds of opportunities."

Husbands Moving for Their Wives

In approximately 10 percent of couple moves, husbands are moving for their wives.[5] This is a phenomenon of recent years, since today more professional women are accepting opportunities for career advancement (including overseas moves) than ever before.[6]

Does a husband experience the same kind of adjustment as a wife when he gives priority to her career goals? We believe that the answer is yes. In fact, some men feel that it may be more difficult because of the added cultural expectations. A typical response is

> We suffer from the same sense of loss and anger, but, in addition, we have to deal with flying in the face of the beliefs that we grew up with, that I, the male, am the breadwinner and the little lady is there for me to protect. This idea is terribly chauvinistic and terribly hard to let go of.

Another man said that he had to put up with a lot of jokes from friends who enjoyed his discomfort: "How does it feel to be a kept man?" "What do you do in your spare time?"[7]

In addition to the loss of his position, one man expressed the fact that his dependency needs increased with the move. "She was the only ongoing, stable relationship in my life." While a woman's spouse may be her best friend, she is more likely than he to have other special confidants, even if she must contact them long distance.

Sometimes a husband moves for his wife because of an earlier agreement to "take turns with our careers." This promise is easier to verbalize than to live out. Debts for a previous move can be hard to pay when the time comes.

One man felt that equity did not necessarily mean a "turn about." He had adjusted well to several moves for his wife's career.

> Both partners should weigh their respective careers, positioning within the field, and the opportunities for each. Usually one or the other, rarely both, is a "golden cow." That person should be given free reign to develop his or her career.

Men find that there are many benefits in moving for their wives—taking a break from the career-ladder syndrome; putting himself on the line for women's rights (to which he has given lip-service); knowing himself to be a trend-setter; and strengthening the marital relationship.[8] A wife is impressed to realize that her husband cares enough to move for her and has little or no resentment when it is her turn to move. Said one respondent, "He has also moved for me. Our relationship is really based on equity."

A couple of women experienced anxiety when their husbands moved for them. They were afraid that their husbands were not going to find satisfying jobs or be happy with the move. One career woman expressed surprise at some of the feelings that surfaced after her husband moved for her benefit.

> I found myself experiencing feelings that a lot of men must feel. I was angry that I was supporting him and that he wasn't pulling equal weight financially. It felt like an enormous amount of responsibility. Very scary. I hadn't expected such a reaction.

Obviously, our society has a long way to go before it will accept as a norm a man moving for his wife's career. Words of advice came from several of our interviewees. They are summarized in a statement by a recent mover: "People do not understand my leaving and my husband's following. I worried that we might be making a mistake. You need to talk through all the angles and ignore what other people say you should do."

Flexible Plans with Dual Careers

Sometimes, dual-career couples feel that no relocation plan looks good. As mentioned previously, ideally a philosophy of transfer should be determined early in the marriage. However, when a specific situation arises, there are usually alternatives. Cathleen Maynard and Robert Zawacki compiled an excellent list of options that we have adapted and elaborated on below.*

1. Alternate which career takes precedence, while recognizing that there will be cycles of opportunity because of the job market and economic reality.

2. When an opportunity to move arises, take a balance sheet approach. List the advantages and disadvantages for each partner separately and for the relationship as a whole. The decision making instrument in chapter 2 can be useful for this purpose.

3. If one partner has generalized skills and can relocate almost anywhere, go where the opportunities are best for the spouse with specialized skills. A move to the Boston area, where a husband found an opportunity to teach in his specialty and the wife found immediate employment in her more marketable skills, is a case in point.

4. Alter one person's career goals or modify both. One couple said, "We decided that our marriage was more important than either of us reaching the top of our careers." Another respondent cautioned that the possibility of not moving up a vocational ladder made it doubly important to go where both were *really* happy with their jobs.

5. Reverse traditional roles whereby the man becomes a househusband. One man indicated that he became aware of what some homemakers go through. "My big moment of the day came when I heard my wife's car in the driveway."

6. Work in two cities fairly close together and live at the half-way point, commuting daily from the same home base.

*Adapted from "Organizations Must Meet This Challenge: Is Yours Ready?" by Cathleen Maynard and Robert Zawacki. Copyright © July 1979. Reprinted with the permission of *Personnel Journal,* Costa Mesa, California; all rights reserved.

7. If with a corporation, go to the employer of the voluntary mover with a clear set of goals, and a list of acceptable solutions. Negotiate simultaneously for two positions. A couple with one large firm made a satisfying cross-country move this way. Evidently, men who move for their wives are more aggressive than women in demanding career assistance. Even if the organization does not have a formal program, the men view assistance as their entitlement.[9]

8. Integrate careers by working full time with your spouse, job-sharing or by working in related fields. Company couples and co-pastorates in the ministerial field are becoming popular options.

9. Go separate ways for short-term opportunities. Many "temporary" moves (for example, commuter marriages) are made on this basis.

Commuter Marriages

Commuter marriages are increasingly common and deserve special attention in this chapter. Couples often explore the possibility of a commuter marriage when

both are high in job satisfaction, status, and earning level and neither wants to sacrifice a career;

either partner is in a university program in which the credits are non-transferable;

one partner has been too briefly in a particular job, and a move would not look good on a dossier;

the partner is in a job that offers excellent training and he or she doesn't want to move now;

the mover is unsure whether the new position or location will work out well and wants to give it a try without disrupting the whole family; or when

the children are at a place in their schooling when a move would be unusually difficult for them.

Sometimes reasons for commuting arise from joint custody arrangements. A divorced mother with two children had spent two years commuting to another state to be with her future husband. After their marriage, she then commuted every third week to be with her children, who had remained in the previous town with their father.

On balance, a commuter marriage seems to have more problems than benefits attached to it, as attractive as the possibility may seem at a given time. This is especially true if a temporary arrangement becomes long-term.

Advantages of a Commuter Marriage. The zest of being together after prolonged absences is a real plus. "We drop everything for our time together, focusing totally on each other. It's like a bunch of short honeymoons." A parallel advantage is freedom to invest in an exciting career during the solo periods. In addition, the multiple losses of an undesired move are avoided.

The biggest advantage is the opportunity to maximize potential without sacrificing a significant relationship. There can be a sense of pride in being on the cutting edge of societal change.

Disadvantages of a Commuter Marriage. A commuter marriage can be difficult even though it has been mutually decided upon.

There is the guilt of not going along with a move that a partner wants to make. Also, a lot of time is spent explaining or justifying a commuter marriage to family and friends.
The presence of the loved one is missed when special support is needed, and loneliness is experienced when one is the third wheel at a party.
Colleagues and bosses don't understand plane schedules and the need for flexibility.
It's sometimes difficult to shift gears when coming back together again. Commuters can feel like guests in each others' homes.
For those who have children, single parenthood can be trying, especially for the one with major responsibility.
Travel creates a financial burden and a drain on one's

energy. It's too easy to decide not to make the trip and, therefore, to loosen the marital bond.

Problems and feelings may not be shared openly out of the fear of ruining the short amount of "special time" together. The relationship may become a bit shallow with lots of pent up feelings below the surface.

Eventually, a temporary commuter marriage ends with a reunion. Such a joyous occasion brings its own stress and readjustment problems. Unrealistic expectations can make the homecoming disappointing.

Evaluating the Possibility of a Commuter Marriage

What are the circumstances under which commuter marriages work well despite these disadvantages? To test out the possibility of a commuter marriage, you can review the profile below, compiled from various descriptions of successful commuter couples.[10]

Timing. The best times for a commuter marriage seem to be in the post-honeymoon and empty nest stages of the marriage. (Some question the earlier of these stages, since the relationship may not have had time to achieve stability.) Few couples try a commuter marriage with infants and small children because of the complications of single parenting.

Distance. It's important to live close enough to get together every weekend, or at least every other weekend. Monthly (or less frequent) reunions are stressful. The greater the distance, in terms of travel hours, the more strain on energy and on the relationship.

Temporariness. It is easier to view even a long-term commuter marriage as temporary.

Career. Is there flexibility on the job? Are you both well established in your careers and reasonably successful? Do you accept your partner's career?

Marriage. Have you been married ten years or more? Are you committed to being married in spite of living apart?

Children. Are children involved? Resentment can build up over extended care of children alone. Also, there may be guilt on the part of either parent for putting career ahead of family. Grown children are considered a plus.

Personal Traits. Do you both have a sense of humor? Are you a good organizer, self-confident, and self-reliant? Are you able to delegate responsibility? Does what others think not concern you? Do you have a lot of energy, and are you physically fit?

Shared Characteristics. Can you spend your time together focused on each other and undistracted by work? Do you have many common interests?

Finances. Do you have money for frequent contacts? Be realistic when evaluating the finances. Available money to hire help can free up time to be together.

As you choose how to handle decisions about moving when you are in a dual-career marriage, one of the alternatives mentioned above may appeal to you. Many of the interviewed couples predicted that as women focus increasingly on their careers, discussions regarding relocation will intensify. Searching for alternatives is important.

Homemaker-Career Couples

After my marriage, we moved five times in eight years, and I hated it more each time. The disruption of daily life, the petty chores, like changing addresses, the readjustments were all unbearable—especially with babies and small children to cope with.

In the homemaker-career family, the wife chooses (or feels pressured) to devote herself to making a home for her husband and their children. She views this as her career—at least for the present. It has been estimated that the number of families in which the mother is a full-time homemaker, the father is the single provider, and the children are in school will be as low as 7 percent by the end of the 1980's.[11] According to the latest Bureau of Labor Statistics, the majority of mothers of children younger than one year old are now in the labor force.

For many years, people have believed that moves are no

problem for the homemaker. After all, she has no responsibilities other than to pack up the house and leave. Usually relocation is a cause for celebration. Some real pluses to being a corporate wife or the wife of a professional man on the way up his particular ladder are: pride in his achievements, financial security and material rewards, status, exposure to important people and events, the opportunity to travel, and the chance to give some real advantages to one's children that might otherwise not be available to them.[12]

However, recent studies have found that wives of relocated employees are vulnerable to depression.[13] When a new move is proposed, these women are torn between their own best interests and loyalty to their husbands. In addition, they believe that they have no right to object to the move because they are not bringing money into the family coffers.

Carol Gilligan reports from her research on women and moral decisions that women define themselves in terms of human relationships and their ability to care.[14] Therefore, if they truly believe that a particular move is to the advantage of their husbands, it would go against their values and belief system to say no. "You're caught between a rock and a hard place. You want to support his goals, and yet you are facing something painful to yourself. Marriage is special. If it makes sense, you go!"

Most homemakers are attached to their neighborhood and community far more than are their husbands, or even than employed wives, and relocation can rupture an emotional lifeline. The loss of important friendships, social and family roles, and personal security is both painful and demoralizing. Old routines that give a sense of stability and control in their lives are disrupted.[15] No matter what they do, they feel that the move *will* take place. They cannot influence the direction of their lives. "I did not like feeling helpless in our search for a new location. My husband sent out his resumes, set up his interviews, and so on. It was as if our entire destiny was out of my hands."

Usually, too, the wife is left to settle the children into unfamiliar schools and neighborhoods, to organize the house, and to find friends. Her husband plunges into his new position and she minimizes her right to have problems. Both behaviors contribute to his lack of awareness of her pain.

> Each partner has to take the responsibility to listen to the other person's needs and *talk them out*. Even just saying, "I don't feel that I have a right to these feelings, but . . ." can relieve some of the pressure.

After the move, friends upon whom both have counted over the years are many miles away. It is important to keep in touch with old friends, through telephone calls ("Up goes the phone bill!"), letters, tapes, and even a return visit. In addition, anticipating periods of loneliness and rootlessness can minimize the shock when these times inevitably arise. A word of advice from one of our respondents is

> Don't line up a lot of friends and relatives for visits within the first few months of a move. An onslaught of old friends can be exhausting and can also get in the way of making new ones. Instead, get out and meet the folks in your community and allow time to have fun.

According to many of our interviewees, one way to make new friends is to

> Become active in your local church. Don't just show up once a week and dash home after services, but join some small groups and get to know people. You can enrich the spiritual and social life of the whole family. The adage "Families that pray together, stay together" is statistically true.

Another suggestion is for you to start your own support group. One woman, who is married to a minister, wrote

> I remember standing in my backyard, crying because I was so lonely. The church people were friendly, but they had stuck me on a pedestal alongside my husband. I decided there must be other lonely ministers' wives in the city, so I started a study-support group. It was a great success. Although the group ended after three years (because most of us moved) we are still good friends.

Men also find support groups helpful. Short-term discussion groups, focusing on issues around moving, can be fun for a couple and can give the opportunity for real sharing between partners. Such groups are usually offered through relocation centers, libraries, churches, or counseling centers. Or, again, you may start a group. You should have no problems in finding participants.

Multiple Moves

Whatever a wife's situation—a career, an enjoyable part-time job, or making a career of homemaking—even though promotions are welcome the hassles and loneliness of relocation are not welcome, especially if they come often. Said one multiple mover, "I get tired of always being new and long to meet an old friend or to see a familiar face. Sometimes I think I am riding a run-away horse; it has got to tire out sometime."

For employed wives, frequent moves can result over time in a meaningless series of jobs that are below their training and capability. They begin to feel helpless and hopeless—even demoralized. With each relocation, their chances of enjoying gratifying work in their fields diminish.

> Our system is unfair to women who relocate with their husbands. The moving van drove up the same day I received my state license to practice psychology. Two other moves, and different state credential requirements, have kept me from being relicensed. I don't think I'd even remember now what to do in my profession.

In addition, an investment of energy, hope, and enthusiasm is required to see consistently each move as an opportunity and a challenge. It is hard to view a move as a challenge after too many changes and lost career opportunities. The wife may begin to feel drained and apathetic.

> Starting over once more hit me hard. We had made so many short-term moves, and I suddenly realized how far I was from my comfort zone—home, parents, long-term friends, associates, my musical life. I felt lost; I had no sense of identity.

Some women make occupational choices in the hope of finding a career that will be reasonably easy to transfer from one part of the country to another—for example, nursing and teaching. One of our respondents indicated that she had a bookkeeping degree. For her, this particular training traveled well, and she had been able to get satisfying jobs in the communities to which she and her family had moved. Flexibility is especially useful when there are frequent moves.

To help combat the feeling of rootlessness, one suggestion for multiple movers who can afford it is to find even a tiny summer place to which one can go yearly; it offers roots for the whole family. A military wife indicated that such a place made a huge difference to her family.

When many moves have been made, sometimes horror stories get passed down through the generations. A woman who moved seventeen times in nineteen years wrote:

> In our worst move, we arrived the day before the movers. We spent the night camping on the floor of our rented house. At eight-thirty in the morning, the moving van backed into the steep driveway. The driver got out to check his position; the brakes failed; and the truck rolled down the driveway and into the kitchen of our brand-new house!

Despite the concerns we hear expressed about multiple moves, one woman began to appreciate them in their absence.

> I had been looking forward to settling in one place and putting down roots. However, after three years in the same community, I found myself getting restless. Much to my surprise, I missed the "fix" of a move, the freshness of the new adventure.

Resistance to Moving

Many husbands realize how difficult moves may be for their families and themselves and are beginning to talk back when their companies tell them to relocate. Some men indicated to us that specific moves have been extremely painful for them. "I expected to feel some torn edges with a move, but in leaving this place and the job I created I felt as if I were mourning the death of my child."

Corporations are revealing a sharp increase in the number of employees refusing to transfer. Apparently, one-third to one-half of the employees who are asked to move now object.[16] Management can no longer assume that faithful employees will unquestionably obey their directives. The earlier definition of company loyalty (as reflected in the following quotation from an Atlanta executive) is changing:

> If [an individual] turns down a promotional opportunity more than once or twice, his career is ended. My own personal feeling is that a man should have dominance over his wife just to say, "We're moving." If he doesn't have the dominance over his wife, he doesn't have the leadership ability we want.[17]

Corporations are responding to their employees' reluctance to leave. Because companies risk losing employees if they pressure them to move, some are trying to promote employees within the local organizational structure. The development of relocation plans is another response. Corporations that have sufficiently large staffs have their own in-house relocation departments. Smaller businesses use relocation companies that specialize in moving executives. Assistance ranges from brochures about the new location to therapy for over-stressed families and even travel games for the kids.

Those corporations that offer services to the wife employed outside the home may help her find a job in the same company, circulate her resume in a new area, join regional consortiums that establish job banks that list available positions in a new area, pay spouses' job hunting expenses, and even hire an outside consultant to work with the spouse.[18] These companies find an unexpected benefit in the deep appreciation of these efforts whether or not anything works out for the spouse.

However, there is still a gap between what is possible and what has been attained. When assigning relocation funds, most companies consider family concerns to be luxury items. Yet, unsuccessful moves prove costly since a company transfer ranges from twenty-five thousand dollars to as much as forty-two thousand dollars.

Empathy

Whether in a dual career or one career family, the most important factor for couples who are moving is shared understanding of the special physical and psychological disruption of a move. The one who instigates the move may feel considerable guilt, discomfort, and helplessness when the family struggles to adjust to the move. Satisfaction with the new position and location is *strongly* influenced by the non-voluntary mover. It is difficult for one to concentrate on a new job when faced with a depressed spouse and unhappy children. Personnel managers report that four out of five failed relocations are caused by poor personal and family adjustments. "When the employee's spouse isn't sold on the idea of relocating, it might be better to transfer a different employee."[19]

Whenever a couple relocates, at least three sets of goals are involved: his, hers, and theirs. The more each partner understands the needs and desires of the other, the more the couple will be able to make it *their* move.

> We worked together to choose a city and a house to move to that we would both be happy with and that would provide us both with quality opportunities. Neither of us wanted the other to sacrifice or to suffer inferior opportunities for the other.

Marcel Mauss wrote that the mere pursuit of individual ends is harmful to the peace of the whole, to the rhythm of its work and pleasure, and, in the end, to the individual.[20] Several couples mentioned that mutual understanding was enhanced by the way they handled relocation. "When you love and respect each other without stereotyped roles, you talk and pray, and then decide which of the doors that God has opened you will walk through together."

Putting your relationship with your partner first can bring you closer so that you can share the problems as well as the excitement of a move. This is certainly the goal to be achieved and is an affirmation of mature love.

Notes

1. Lyle Schaller, *It's a Different World* (Nashville: Abingdon Press, 1987), p. 146.

2. A. C. Bebbington, "The Function of Stress in the Establishment of the Dual-Career Family." *Journal of Marriage and the Family* 35 (May 1973): 530.

3. Carol Gilmore and William Fannin, "The Dual Career Couple: A Challenge to Personnel in the Eighties." *Business Horizons* 25 (May-June 1982): 36.

4. Irene Pave, "Move Me, Move My Spouse: Relocating the Corporate Couple." *Business Week* (December 16, 1985):57ff.

5. Carole Gould, "A Helping Hand for the 'Trailing Spouse.'" *New York Times* (February 22, 1987):11.

6. Cathleen Maynard and Robert Zawacki, "Organizations Must Meet This Challenge; Is Yours Ready?" *Personnel Journal* 58 (July 1979): 469.

7. Gordon Mott, "Following a Wife's Move." *New York Times Magazine* (April 14, 1985):58.

8. Ibid.

9. Gould, "A Helping Hand," p. 11.

10. Naomi Gerstel, *Commuter Marriages* (New York: Guilford Press, 1984), chapter 7; Fairlee Winfield, *Commuter Marriage: Living Together, Apart* (New York: Columbia Press, 1985), chapter 7; Lisa Belkin, "When Marriage Is Long Distance." *New York Times* (October 3, 1985):17.

11. Uma Sekaran, *Dual-Career Families* (San Francisco: Jossey-Bass, Inc., 1986), p. 2.

12. "Executive Wives View Marriage as a Combination of Rewards and Sacrifices." *Wall Street Journal* (December 16, 1981): 1.

13. Jeanne Brett, "The Effect of Job Transfer on Employees and Their Families." In *Current Concerns in Occupational Stress,* eds. Cary Cooper and Roy Paine (New York: John Wiley and Sons, 1980), pp. 99-136.

14. Carol Gilligan, *In A Different Voice* (Cambridge: Harvard University Press, 1982).

15. Brett, "The Effect of Job Transfer on Employees and Their Families," p. 100.

16. Maynard and Zawacki, "Organizations," p. 469.

17. Mayanne Vandervelde, "The Corporate Wife." *Across the Board* (March 1979): 30.

18. Barbara Delatiner, "Trailing a Transferred Husband." *Working Mother* 7 (April 1984): 75.

19. Edward Snow, "Spouse's Attitude Influences Move." *Personnel Journal* 63 (November 1984): 30-31.

20. Marcel Mauss, *The Gift* (Glencoe, Ill.: The Free Press, 1954) p. 75; originally published in 1925.

CHAPTER 4

Moving with Children

When we told our eleven-year-old son that we had decided to move to New York from New Jersey, he burst into tears and sobbed, "But it has taken me so long to belong here, and I'll have to start all over again."

The average child moves three times during the school-aged years and feels the impact of a move as intensely as adults. To children, the parents' decision to move is an arbitrary one over which they have no control. They, too, have friends who are dear to them, and separation is hard to understand. They, too, find security in the familiarity of their environment and are threatened by change. They, too, have jobs to do; the work of children—learning about their world—is continuous, intense, and all-absorbing, and it is disrupted by a move.

From infancy to teenage years, children react with strong emotions. They may or may not verbalize what they are experiencing. A fussy six-month-old became sunshine itself when a friend of the parents took her for a day. The baby had been a Geiger counter for adult tensions.

Older children are more able than their younger siblings to hide their feelings, if they really want to. Mr. R's family moved after his business collapsed, and he plunged into depression. His thirteen-year-old son developed severe cramps that went undiagnosed for months. He had kept his grief about the move to himself, out of concern for his father. A move that follows a business failure, divorce, death, or remarriage involves a great deal of adjustment on the part of the whole family and intensifies the problems around relocation.

It is healthier for children who are moving to let their feelings out, even if the parents aren't thrilled to get the message. Lisa, fifteen, let her parents know that they had ruined her social life, jeopardized her grade point average, and had permanently damaged her psyche with "their" move. Another teenager wrote his parents an ugly letter when they moved across town—four blocks. He hadn't been consulted; his friends were still "over there"; the new house wasn't the house he wanted; and his model airplane was lost in the move.[1]

According to children's reports, the worst parts of a move are leaving friends and starting in a new school. The best parts of a move are traveling, learning about a new place, and (paradoxically) going to a new school and making friends. Always, there is gain and loss. "I moved five times as a child. I never liked moving, especially leaving behind friends and pets. However, I do feel it broadened my life."

It is comforting to know that a move does not necessarily have to result in negative long-term effects on children. A periodic move may even be beneficial. Generally children adjust after brief periods of stress and disorganization. According to parents in one study, their children made friends easily (80 percent), the school change was not difficult (75 percent), and in 81 percent of the situations there was either no effect or a positive one.[2]

Of course, this leaves one in four or five children with adjustment problems, and to them and their families they are not percentages. Some children have an exceptionally hard time with a move. Reactions that may be triggered are a drop in academic performance, withdrawal and depression, a desire to run away, drug involvement, and even suicide.[3] There are differences of opinion as to how much relocation affects children's academic achievement, but researchers agree that the children who have the hardest time adjusting are those who are "different" from their classmates in size, age, or culture or those with a physical handicap or poor self-concept.[4] A "cultural difference" could mean being from another part of the country.

The "when" of a move is much discussed in research. Apparently, the time of the year is not a significant factor in children's adjustment. Each season has its advocates. Some say that the fall or summertime is best because the child is not thrust into a new school in the middle of the year. Others suggest spring because classes are well established, teachers take time to integrate a new child into the class, and friendships are formed before summer arrives. One respondent indicated that she didn't like a childhood move in winter. "I was so afraid that Santa Claus wouldn't find me."

Younger Children

Younger children generally enjoy moves more than older ones. An exception may be the four to six year olds who are moving at the same time that they are embarking on their first major separation from home. Adjustment to starting school may be prolonged by a move, especially if there is a learning problem. "I had a very hard time entering first grade after moving to a new community. We were unaware that I was dyslexic, so I had two major adjustments."

Some parents report interrupted sleep patterns of young children or regressive clinging; others talk of rapid adjustment.

> My four-year-old was initially excited about the move, but quickly began missing his backyard, preschool, and friends. He's not shy and makes friends easily, so he has overcome these losses.

Contrary to what one might think, it's unwise to farm young children out during relocation—even to grandparents. Research on mother-child relationships indicates that separation at a time of change can have negative long-term results.[5] Children need to go through the steps of the move with the rest of the family. Jobs, such as packing toys, can make them feel included. Taking along the children's (and the parents') favorite sitter for a month can provide continuity for the children and can be a real blessing to the parents as they unpack.

Adolescents

> Our two older children view "home" as where they used to live. They feel as if we've run away from home and are visiting rather than living here.

Moves are particularly difficult for teenagers. The task of adolescence is to establish a unique identity separate from parents. From psychosocial theory, we learn that self-concept develops through children's interaction within their social setting and that continuity supports a healthy sense of identity.[6] Establishing close and lasting relationships with peers is crucial, so losing one's friends is personally disruptive.

In addition, firm cliques are commonly found in the new high school, and the breaking-in process is difficult. If one is "different" (even coming from another part of the country) the adjustment can be painful. You can figure out how to be "cool" in one part of the country and find that those rules don't apply elsewhere.

> Bobby socks were in where I came from and out where I went. Also, my Texas accent set me apart in California. Instead of being head cheerleader, as I was slated to be back home, I wasn't even on the team. The worst part was that my parents paid no attention to my misery.

No one welcomes a new kid. An adolescent has to be pretty gregarious to push into already established space. It's no wonder that teenagers are reluctant to move. Says one author, "Teenagers say 'no' for a living, and they can hang their rebellion on the move."[7]

Parents can be understanding

> As the children have gotten into junior high and high school, moving has become more difficult for them. They used to see

moves as adventures. Now they want secure, stable friendships. We are trying hard to stay in this location.

However, the chance for new beginnings may be welcomed by some teens. Brad, thirteen, tried on an outgoing personality; he also abandoned homework. Cindy, sixteen, had been embarrassed by a late puberty, but she blossomed over the summer before entering her new school. "I was now grown-up, and my new friends never knew I'd been a joke before!" A thirteen-year-old boy, after being initially resentful, took the opportunity of the move to make new friends—especially girls.

Sometimes, the "new me" doesn't happen. "You take yourself with you," said one woman, who suffered a traumatic experience in an eleventh grade move. She believes she has never fully recovered from that move.

There is probably no worse time to move than before the senior year of high school. By then, most young people have established some sense of personal identity and a place in the social scheme. If "getting there" has been a hard-won victory, moving can seem tragic. A seventeen-year-old girl reported:

> I had reached *all* of my goals. I had been elected a club president and school representative to the mayor's office. I was on the debating team, a cheerleader, and played on the basketball squad. I had joined the computer/math and Spanish clubs. I was headed for academic honors in my senior year.

Her parent's motive for moving—a nicer house in a different community—must have seemed strange indeed. Yet this girl showed remarkable maturity. She decided "for the betterment of myself" to take things day by day. In her new setting, she was friendly, but concentrated on preparing for college rather than battling her way into the school cliques. "By midyear, people began to know me and to seek me out. I proved to myself that I could make something disappointing into a positive experience instead of a failure."

Much can be learned from this girl. She made use of some

of the coping mechanisms used most often by adolescents: working at maintaining current functioning; introspection; establishing supportive relationships and friendships; formulating a new beginning.[8] (There will be considerably more on coping and coping skills in chapter 8.)

If one has a teenager, especially one close to graduation, considering alternatives to moving is important. One high school student, whose parents didn't move far away, became a commuter. He stayed over with old friends and saved any left-over commute money for parties. "The experience offered a taste of pre-college liberation."

All Ages

Children need to know about a projected move before the extended family and friends are told. Learning about something so personally relevant from persons other than parents can be quite a shock. A three-month notice (if possible) allows the child to get used to the idea. One way *not* to tell a child about a move was described by a boy who discovered that he was moving when he saw a "For Sale" sign on the front lawn upon coming home from school. As indicated in our chapter on decision making, it is important for all children to have input from the beginning, and, when possible, they should be involved in the selection of a new home.

Parents can lesson the confusion of a child at the time of a move by preparing him or her for what to expect of relocation. Sharing information about the new house or apartment, the school, and the community is helpful. The children will ask many questions, which require a patient response. Parents should also ask questions to find out how their children interpret relocation. Amy, four, worried about how the movers could fit her big house in the van. Joey, thirteen, gave up hope that his divorced parents would reunite when they sold the family home. Whatever their age, children see home and family as intertwined.

The most important questions are generally not verbalized: "What is happening to me?" "Am I safe?" and "Who will take care of me?"[9] Parents need to know how their children are coping with mounting anxiety. This is a time for understanding and support. A good children's library has books about moving that are suitable for various ages. Read together by parents and child, these tap into emotions that need to be brought to awareness and discussed. Storytelling can help as well; you don't need to be an expert to work out a simple plot about a child who is moving and who feels anxious.

Special care is needed to hear children describe what they want in order to create a favorite room or their own space in the new home. One father told us that, as soon as they saw the new house, his children claimed as their own the empty room above the garage, shared, as they discovered, by a family of raccoons.

Little is done to help children leave their schools. A few services would be relatively easy to implement: The school from which the child is moving could call the new school and, also, take time to talk to the parents about issues related to their children's adjustment; the children themselves could be encouraged to discuss their concerns about the move and about making new friends; classmates could participate in a study of the region of the country to which the child is going, choose going-away mementos, and give their friend a positive send-off.[10]

Parents can supply cookies and punch for a good-bye party if their child's school doesn't take this kind of initiative. Most teachers would be happy to include this in the school day shortly before the move takes place.

Farewells are important: A ninety year old man looked back at his family's move from a farm to the city when he was four.

> My brother and I bade farewell to the foal and to our three cows in the stable and to the calves, tenderly embracing each one. Finally, we ended up at the pig pen where we both kissed the huge sow, who put her snout obligingly above the bars of her pen. As we started down the lane for the main road, we stood in the back of the wagon, shouting farewells. "Good-bye, cows and horses. Good-bye, cats. Good-bye,

mice. Good-bye, house. Good-bye, barn. Good-bye, trees. Good-bye, hens. Good-bye, grass. Good-bye, everything."

These little boys had expressed their separation from the animals that had populated their lives and from the environs that they had known and loved. They were ready to move on.

After relocation, parents can help their children find new friends and settle into their new community. "My son was so focused on trying to make friends that he let his schoolwork slide. I gave a party for the local children so that he could get acquainted. Now he is putting energy into learning."

Choosing a School

School is second only to family as the most important social setting for children. It is there that children learn the norms and values of the community to which they have moved. Usually, a major family priority is education and, for some families, school quality may determine which residence is selected. Those who rent for awhile before moving into something more permanent, should try to get a place in the school district in which they eventually expect to live. It will save another loss of friends for their children.

It is not easy to identify the neighborhood school system that best meets family expectations. An article by Frank Morin suggests questions to keep in mind when renting or buying a home if a child is to go to a public school. These same questions may be used when selecting a private school (although the house location may be less important, depending on transportation availability and distance). The list below and talking to school personnel and neutral parties can be helpful in assessing the situation. Realtors may be knowledgeable, though perhaps biased.

1. How does the per-pupil expenditure of the school compare with that of other schools in the neighborhood and state?
2. What is the average class size? The maximum class size?

3. How do the pre-college scores compare to the national average?
4. What are the graduation requirements?
5. What percentage of students go on to a four-year college?
6. How many graduates are accepted into highly selective colleges?
7. What are the support services—guidance, social workers, speech and hearing, remedial reading?
8. What are the programs for the gifted, physically handicapped, learning disabled, and intellectually handicapped?
9. Are there any enrichment programs—art, music, drama, computer education?
10. How about sports and extra-curricular activities?
11. What is the accreditation status (if the school is private)?*

One respondent suggested checking with local youth counseling agencies and the police department to determine the drug record of a particular school. That's not generally advertised by the Chamber of Commerce!

A valid question to ask is, "What does the school do to welcome a new child?" Understanding and acceptance by teachers is important to adjustment, according to several of our respondents. A college professor told us: "My first move at seven was very traumatic. The teacher did not welcome new students. I didn't fit in because I didn't know the rules of the school and of her class. She made fun of me."

A young woman who had moved to the United States from Central America had exactly the same experience in the first grade. The teacher tormented the girl because she couldn't speak English, and she was terrified to go to school. The memory, many years later, still brings much pain.

Some schools take the adjustment problems of children seriously. A school counselor interviews children when they

*Adapted from Frank Morin, "How to Select a School System." Copyright © November 1984. Reprinted with the permission of *Personnel Journal*, Costa Mesa, California; all rights reserved.

arrive to determine the best class setting for each child. A follow-up interview about two weeks later ensures a good placement. Progressive schools also offer an introductory meeting with the parents, the child, someone from the administration, and the child's teacher. They may also have a "buddy" system to introduce the child to the other students, to help her or him find a locker, and escort the child to lunch (one of the more terrifying experiences for a new child). Catch-up tutoring during the year, a "welcoming club," and materials for a prospective student—such as the names, positions, and phone numbers of school personnel, a floor map, a student handbook, a schedule of extracurricular activities and how to join them, a list of community activities, and possibly some free passes to events in the school and in the community—may be offered as well.[11] These are all suggestions that may be implemented by those on P.T.A. Boards in order to make moves easier for children.

Coping with a Move

Healthy family relationships are the most significant stabilizing influence in a move. Children need extra time with understanding parents who can emphasize that the whole family is experiencing the readjustment together. Keeping up with ongoing traditions and normal schedules (such as Sunday morning pancakes) before and after the move promotes feelings of security. The arrival of familiar furniture and the restoration of order also helps.

A parent with a positive outlook can help the child view the move as a challenge. For example, necessarily brief temporary moves might be framed as vacations to ease the adjustment process. Unfortunately, however, at the time of a move, parents may distance themselves because they are dealing with their own feelings. Father may be anxious about his new position and working overtime. Mother may be upset about the move. The child may suffer not only the loss of familiar surroundings, but the loss of parenting as well. In order to guard against this happening, special awareness of its possibility is important.

Evidently, children with siblings have less trouble adjusting to a move than do only children. Leaving a sibling behind, however, is very difficult. This can happen if a teenager remains with a grandparent or a close friend to finish high school or if siblings are separated by custody arrangements.

Other Issues

When a child's best friend moves, attention focuses on the one who is leaving, not on the child who remains behind, feeling abandoned.

> One of the most traumatic experiences of my life was when my best friend moved. We were twelve at the time and real soulmates. We played guitars and sang together. We understood each other in a way no one else could. It took me years to get over the loss.

When a special friend moves away, a child's feelings deserve to be heard. The child could be facing a very lonely experience. The person counted on for special events, to eat lunch with, to talk to by the hour will no longer be available. Sadness for the loss and the anxiety of trying to find someone else to fill the void can be overwhelming. A child who does not make friends easily may find such an experience devastating.

Moving may be difficult for children at first, but most of them make a good adjustment after a brief period, usually less than a year. Parents who are sensitive to a child's moods and are open to hearing anything that indicates problems can help immeasurably with the settling-in process. A joyous experience was reported by one of our respondents.

> I remember living in a rented house while my father built a home for us across town. We moved in long before it was finished. We roller-skated on the concrete floors. My mom did all the inside painting; my dad built all the cabinets; and we children did things like collect and straighten nails. Everyone was part of the experience!

A reasonable number of childhood moves (considered by some researchers to be two or three) offer opportunities for growth for the child. Moves increase social skills, flexibility, and independence and provide experiences of the country and even of the world. Such children learn to handle themselves in a variety of situations and are not usually as threatened by change as children who never have the opportunity to move.

"I loved moving as a child. My parents always put it in terms of an adventure. For me, even as an adult, every move has been a positive experience." This attitude would be quite a gift to give to children. This is a reciprocal situation in that children are, also, an asset to parents in the adjustment to a move. Making friends with peers, they expose adults to other families and may be a comforting distraction from feelings of loss.

Notes

1. Theresa Byrne-Dodge, "When Children Are Moved." *American Way* (October 15, 1986):92.

2. Curtis Barrett and Helen Noble, "Mothers' Anxieties Versus the Effects of Long-distance Moves on Children." *Journal of Marriage and the Family* 35 (May 1973):181.

3. Byrne-Dodge, "When Children Are Moved," pp. 92-94.

4. Thomas Cornille, Alan Bayer, and Charlotte Smyth, "New Schools and Newcomers: A National Survey of Innovative Programs." *Personnel and Guidance Journal* 62 (December 1983):231.

5. Robert Stubblefield, "Children's Emotional Problems Aggravated by Family Moves." *Journal of Orthopsychiatry* 25 (1955):120.

6. Jane Kroger, "Residential Mobility and Self Concept in Adolescence." *Adolescence* 15 (Winter 1980):967.

7. Jane Mitchell, "Expert Helps Dispel Some Myths About Moving Experience." *The Oregonian* (April 26, 1985):E17.

8. Kevin Donohue and Thomas Gullotta, "The Coping Behavior of Adolescents Following a Move." *Adolescence* 18 (Summer 1983):396.

9. Louise Beem and Diane Prah, "When I Move Away, Will I Still Be Me?" *Childhood Education* 60 (May-June 1984):310.

10. Cornill, Bayer, and Smyth, "New Schools," p. 235.

11. Ibid., pp. 231ff.

CHAPTER 5

Singles on the Move

I needed to move to become a full-fledged adult. I had a chance to reach for my dreams and make them come true. Rather than distress, a move is merely change, and both sadness and joy always come with change.

There are approximately fifty-six million single adults in the United States today. More than two-thirds do not live alone, and this percentage continues to climb. Most single adults live with a friend, with a lover, or with a relative. By 1990, the prediction is that there will be a single adult in one out of every four households.[1] In this chapter on singles and moving, we will explore several different kinds of moves: moves to go to college, moves for work, moves for relationships, and moves after a divorce.

Moves to Go to College

Going to college was my very first move and a positive experience. I was excited about the freedom of leaving home and being on my own.

When a young person goes off to college or leaves home for a job, only one family member moves; everyone else stays behind. Attention is focused on the mover and the new experiences that lie ahead. However, the transition to college affects two generations. As their children move toward independence, parents are relinquishing an important and challenging role. For both parents and children, the experience is exciting and scary, fraught with the ambivalence of letting go and of hanging on.

The process of separation begins many years earlier than when leaving home. A mother's body—"home" for nine months—prepared itself to release new life. Individuation continues as parents and children move toward eventually divergent paths. Each stage builds on the success of the last one.

During the first three years of life, children achieve a sense of confidence in themselves and in their parents so that times of separation are accepted as normal rather than as threatening events. Going to school is another major change for the growing child. This can and should be a positive event if the first separation process went well and if there are no traumatic life events at that time. The child learns how to relate to teachers and to peers and how to balance these two experiences—school and home—while coping with a widening world.

In adolescence, the separation process continues when those involved prepare realistically for changes to come. Social psychologists call this preparation (on the part of both child and parent) anticipatory socialization. The process usually starts earlier for boys than for girls in our society. Often there are rehearsals for independence for college bound young people. Some spend a couple of summer weeks traveling with a friend's family. Others get summer jobs out of town, perhaps living with relatives who have children of a similar age. A few fortunate young people have the opportunity while still in high school for a year abroad through Rotary Club, American Field Service organization, or some other group. At about this time, these young people begin to view college students (especially older siblings) as models for their future.

Undercurrents of change can cause powerful reactions. One young man said:

> In my senior year of high school, I thought a lot about death—mine and my parents. Mom explained that I was dealing with separation from home as I planned for college. That made a lot of sense and helped get my feelings into perspective.

Shifts in the family system mean adjustments for everyone involved, not just for the young adult. Family members, aware or not of what they are doing, anticipate changes. Parents will have more time for each other and for their individual interests. The next sibling in line will become the oldest one at home with all the responsibilities and privileges implied. The family circle begins to open, making space to launch one of its own into the larger world.

One way parents can help their children to achieve independence in their growing years is by gradually giving them age-appropriate tasks that increase freedom of decision and activity. When semi-independence is experienced in advance, the unrestricted liberties of college—so appealing and yet so frightening—are easier to handle.

Especially if the process of separation-individuation has not been satisfactorily completed, the leave taking can be extremely traumatic for both the parents and the child. Unfortunately, as college looms closer, some parents start placing more demands, rather than less, on the child they are about to lose. In turn, the young person may become increasingly strident in proclaiming independence. Distrust and resentment build when distorted messages are received. Both generations are really saying, "This is not easy. I'm afraid of losing you." This is an important feeling and one that should be communicated more directly and honestly.

Occasionally, powerful pressures from home propel young people off to college. They talk of "surviving" or "enduring" family life until they can "get away." Instead of taking only favorite tapes and pictures, they escape with everything they own. Troubled young people often carry their problems with them, complaining of "Nazi supercop" authorities at the college, where they had hoped to be free from rules.

Other students have parents who were recently divorced, and the sale of the family house may signal loss of all hope that one's parents will ever get back together. Such young adults feel, literally as well as figuratively, that there's no "home" to go back to.

Alternatively, home may be too comfortable. One young

man couldn't face the reality until the last minute. "I didn't prepare myself. I was leaving the security of the home I'd always lived in, so it was especially difficult. I hid behind my feelings 'til the night before I left, and then I cried."

According to the students we surveyed, bringing a bit of home to college makes the transition easier. Their special choices, beyond bare necessities, are individual and revealing. Pictures of family and posters of favorite entertainers made their section of a dorm room homey. A guitar or baseball souvenirs—"so much a part of who I am"—broke the ice with new friends. It is interesting to realize how consciously students prepared for feelings of insecurity, down moods, or the need to feel comforted by bringing favorite tapes, books, and stuffed animals.

Identity was packed into suitcases along with favorite sweaters. "I brought my high school yearbooks, soccer pictures, and all the other memorabilia that gave me a sense of belonging and knowing what I could accomplish."

Some college students stretch home ties rather than break them. Having an old friend spend the weekend in the dorm and taking new friends home to meet the family create reassuring bonds in both directions. Phone calls from college and letters from home (it seldom works the other way around) help smooth the transition. These are trying times, and it is good to feel the support of home and family. There is comfort also in the recognition that other students share the anxiety of embarking on a college career.

It is natural to feel ambivalence just before and after the move. The pluses and minuses are often mirror images of each other. One young woman expressed this paradox when she wrote: "What I most dreaded about college was being lonely, and what I most looked forward to was living away from my parents."

"Coming home" for the first time, often for Thanksgiving or Christmas, may be experienced with the same ambivalence. *In*dependence is cherished at college, but it also means taking responsibility and paying at least part of your own way. *Inter*dependence is valued at home, but it is hard to grow up without going away.

Students return to family get-togethers, old friends, home-cooked meals, and free laundry. There is the good feeling of knowing that you've been missed. It is fun getting admiration from younger brothers and sisters and seeing how much they have grown in the few months that have elapsed. These special bonds to family and friends continue to make home meaningful.

Coming home has problems, too. College is a major step in the maturation of young people. Within the first few months or year, significant changes take place. It is hard to be adult-to-adult in the same setting as they were so recently child-to-parent. Old rules and talk of finances and grades are especially jarring as ties to home are reactivated for the almost-adult young person.

College students feel out of touch when faced with changes that have occurred in the family during their absence. Their bedroom may have been translated into a study or a storage room. Perhaps it has even been rented. It is a shock to the person if he or she has had no mention of the plans in advance. "I felt displaced when I returned to find everything of mine packed away. I had to sleep on the couch like a visitor. It wasn't really my home anymore."

Few families can reserve a room for a young person who may only be home for a few days at a time. They are hard pressed for space and frequently assume that changes will be made without discussing them in advance. It is important to let the college student know about prospective changes.

Some students are less attached to a particular room than to the house as a whole. For them, changes are taken in stride. They come back to pleasant memories and to parents who give them the feeling that home is always there for them. The household has an easy give and take atmosphere, mutual acceptance of family members, and an open door policy. These lucky students talked of vacations in which there were big family get-togethers for Thanksgiving and Christmas or in which they enjoyed relaxing and lazing around the house—overdosing on televised football games with friends and relatives. When these young people told us that they lived in the college dorm, they frequently added, "and at my parents' home."

Parents sometimes delay an intended move so that a high school senior doesn't have to change schools. As soon as college starts, they relocate, forgetting that returning for vacation to an unfamiliar house in an unfamiliar location will also be difficult. One young man wrote:

> My parents moved from New York to Philadelphia the fall I went away to college. There was no anchor called "home" to think about while I was getting used to college. I felt I had nothing to come home to, since I did not know anyone, and the house was also new to me.

We are not implying that necessary changes should again be put on hold for the sake of the returning family member. However, parents can exchange ideas in advance, taking into account the concerns of a returning student as well as their own needs. Some kind of satisfying compromise can be made. Vacation may involve the fun of hitting the high spots of a new community together.

Where there is mutual respect, appreciation, caring, and willingness to allow young people to be separate human beings, the parent-child bond is gradually replaced with a deep sense of friendship.

Work-motivated Moves

Singles who move for employment are at one of two stages: leaving home for their first full-time job or moving after their careers have been established. To many of our respondents, the first job was also the first time away from the security of home and school. If they saw their lives to date as fairly successful, they were excited. If they lacked confidence, the plunge into employment was often terrifying. "Looking for a job and a potential move puts me out into the world, and there is no one there to catch me if I fall."

An additional adjustment for some women is the expectation that they will not need to find a vocation or be self-supporting. Their childhood dream was to be married soon after finishing high school or, if college bound, by the time of graduation. By their mid-twenties, they expected that their new family would be established with the birth of one or two children.

Such dreams are perceived by many woman as unacceptable because of the emphasis on individuality and finding a niche in the career world. Those people who have the dream often admit to their fantasies with some embarrassment. If expectations have not materialized, they are at an important transition—trying to decide where to live and how to support themselves for the next few years or perhaps indefinitely. "Do I continue to live at home and find a job locally, or do I take the leap to a city far from home and make a new beginning?"

Although this is usually a difficult decision, most of our respondents (both men and women) who moved away from the home town said that the change was good for them. "I got to know myself as a unique person. I deliberately moved far enough away from my parents to sever the umbilical cord."

A second kind of a job related move comes after a person is established in an occupation and either chooses to move or is moved by a corporation. A chosen move may be precipitated by boredom, the desire for a new beginning, or because of a position that has unexpectedly presented itself. An artist moved to find the truly creative part of herself: "The move was successful; my art became an inner landscape instead of an outer one." A professor moved, even though he loved his teaching position, because he was unable to tolerate the values of the city in which he had lived: "I was *radically* uncomfortable in that community. It was definitely a personal decision to move—not a professional one."

Singles have fewer ties than do families, so there are more "instant movers" among singles. A young man said, "The decision to move to New Orleans was instantaneous. I remained here and called my former employer to quit my job." His family sent his belongings later. A woman was able to grasp her chance without consulting others. "A particularly nasty boss, changes in my community (friends were moving out), and a job possibility that I really wanted came together."

Some people move and keep a foot in both places in order to see what happens. A single man said, "I never changed my address. Everything was forwarded, and I kept my old license plate. I didn't let go in case it didn't work out. Then I could go back home. Holding on was my safety net."

Some singles view this as the time of their lives when they can move abroad and do some things that they might be unable to do later if they have a spouse or children to consider. Some of the chosen positions were teaching English or other subjects for the United States government or for a foreign government, working for the Red Cross, working for a corporation as a specialist abroad, and so on. One woman worked for and traveled extensively with the Federal Bureau of Investigation. A young man said:

> This is the time that I can do anything I want to vocationally. I have always felt a pull to work in a Third World country. If I was in a relationship, my partner might not want to do that, so now is the time to fulfill that dream.

Singles who move by choice may perceive the world as their oyster, but those who are casually relocated by their companies feel a good deal of resentment. The attitude of most corporations is evidenced by the fact that single men have higher mobility than do married men.[2] The singles are piqued that they are considered "easy moves" because they often don't have houses and families that tie them to a particular city. The fact that they may have a special someone and a network of personal and professional friends is not taken into account. It often takes a long time in a new location to find quality friendships. One man indicated that he had left an excellent position because of the probability that he would have to move once he became a partner in the corporation. The shift may be especially hard for single women who aren't readily accepted into the "inner circle" of male peers.[3]

Whether moves have an auspicious beginning or not often

depends on the employer. Two quite different scenarios were described by our interviewees. One woman said that her new employer informed her about what she might expect, toured the city with her, and included her in some social events. Another employee of a different corporation said: "I was told to rent a car and drive around Los Angeles. There is nothing worse than being lost in a big city with no one to guide you."

Because of the number of large companies that are moving out of cities, many singles in recent years have been making the move to the suburbs. This change is evidenced by some suburban churches that have weekly groups of singles, numbering in the hundreds.

Moves for Relationships

Many men and women move in order to test a relationship to see whether it can develop into a permanent one. As with married couples who move for their relationships, singles find that this kind of move can result in a job below their potential. If the relationship doesn't work out, that person may be left in the cold to make another move and, in addition, to repair a shattered ego. However, a happy ending is possible.

I moved for my boyfriend and also because I was bored with the job and the life-style where I was living. I wanted a new beginning with him at my side. Even though the relationship broke up, I still consider it the best move I've made. It is the slams against the ego that ultimately strengthen it—like exercise for the body.

Another woman almost *didn't* make the move for her boyfriend: "I almost resisted moving because it seemed so cliché, 'moving for my man's career.' Grr . . .I hated the idea that I might be sacrificing my career or my image. But as time passed, my anger faded, and I realized I could grow from the move myself."

Men can have the same concern about moving for a

partner, although, as with married couples, the additional problem is that the move goes against societal stereotypes instead of with them.

> If I move for Jean it looks as if she has the upper hand in the relationship. Actually, I know that isn't true, but that's how it feels, and I think that's how others would view it.

Relationship moves may come from the desire to be with a best friend. Some who think they may be too lonely convince friends to move with them so that they will have a built-in support system; it usually is not too difficult to convince a best friend to move, since it is not fun to be left behind. "It is definitely easier to move with someone rather than alone . . . as long as the relationship continues to be good."

Sometimes a move to "find oneself" or to pursue a career causes a break in a relationship. A woman who moved to an art center to pursue her work had to leave her lover behind because of the difficulty of reestablishing a private practice as a therapist in a distant city. Choices like this one are hard to make. If you are not absolutely certain of the future of the relationship, you might not feel that you can sacrifice a career. Nevertheless, as one man put it, "It's hard to be alone, functioning as a single person and not having the support. Pervasive loneliness can destroy otherwise strong people."

Whether you make a relationship move or a job related move, the most crucial factor is that you feel that you are making the move for yourself and are not making an enormous sacrifice for someone else or for the corporation. That kind of move backfires in built-up resentment, which is apt to spill out in destructive ways. The move needs to be viewed as *"my choice."*

> The best move I ever made was prompted by my own motives and my own decisions. I wanted to be there in that location at that particular time.

Divorce and Single Parents

When making a new start, one of the biggest adjustments is the anxiety about the safety and sounds in an urban

community. I made the transition from suburbs to city, house
to condo, and supermom to single adult.

A potentially traumatic move is one at the time of a divorce.
This is true whether the mover is the instigator of the divorce
or the partner who is being left. At this time, one is
particularly vulnerable to psychological and physical symptoms. Plans that have been built, perhaps since childhood,
crash and burn. Even under the best of circumstances, there
may be feelings of failure, guilt, sadness, and anger. "I was
mourning the things around which I had woven dreams and
dealing with the fact that all were aborted. I felt incomplete,
unfinished, and sad."

Severe financial stress compounds these problems. One or
both partners must, of necessity, move at the time of divorce.
There is no denying the fact that two households cost a great
deal more than one. Local moves may mean a smaller
apartment or house and the loss of role and status. Dark
basement flats exacerbate depression and a sense of loss.
Any move should be made to a cheerful setting, even though
it may be small. As a woman in her forties explained:

> My best and worst moves were within the same house. I had
> built my home and lived in it for twelve years, renting out the
> basement flat. When my finances crashed at the time of my
> divorce, I rented out my part of the house and moved into the
> basement.

Although this was a local move—even in the same
building—it expressed the enormous pain that comes with
such a loss of status. Just to wake up was to be reminded of
the situation; to be in the basement instead of the upper
floors was symbolic of where she saw herself.

A move at the time of a divorce can be a positive experience
if the relationship was strained and one wanted to be out of it.
The recognition of being able to "survive, adjust, and
rebuild" was personally affirming to a divorced man. Also, a
woman who had taken twenty years to leave a bad marriage
wrote:

Toward the end I dreamed that I was swimming desperately out of a swirling vortex. My first evening in my tiny apartment I had neither furniture nor electricity. Special friends came over, and we sat on pillows, drinking champagne by candlelight. I was my own person at last.

Frequent moves can be the precipitating factor in a divorce, leading, therefore, to one more move. If the relationship is already strained, the announcement of another move may trigger one partner (frequently the wife) to decide to leave. This is especially true if she has a career and the move means starting over one more time.

We had made three moves in less than four years. This time we had already put a downpayment on a new house, and, once again, I was going to have to look for a job. One morning I just said, "I'm not going."

Another woman said that her husband's unilateral decision to move from the East to the West Coast was a precipitating factor in their divorce.

I was not consulted on the last of our many moves. I loved my job, but my husband hated his. During a job hunting trip, he wired me a bouquet of roses. The attached note said, "Off to our new adventure. Love, J." He had decided without even phoning me!

Decisions of whether to move to another city or to another part of the country at the time of a divorce depend on several issues.

1. Is the break-up viewed as permanent? One woman indicated that she made several temporary moves in the same area in the hope that her marriage could be salvaged.

2. How often has the person moved previously? For frequent movers, relocation may be a way of coping with stress. Divorce will trigger another move.

3. What about social support systems? These affect decisions around moving at the time of a divorce. Even one good friend is an enormous comfort after a divorce—with the

feelings of grief and anger, the responsibilities of children, the tension over custody, and the two-in-the-morning loneliness. A divorced man said: "One friend would call and ask how I was doing. If I sounded down he'd say, 'Wind up your work and I'll meet you in half an hour.' You can't find those kinds of friends easily—and you certainly don't give them up."

Persons who are surrounded by family and friends are unlikely to move away, but if there is no local support group, serious consideration is given to moving closer to the family of origin.

4. Who has the children? The custodial parent usually tries to remain in the house for a minimal disruption of the children's lives. Moving with unhappy children at the time of a divorce can be a disaster. For some of our respondents, the move, if it was made, was followed within months by the unhappy child's return to the original hometown to live with the other parent. That proves to be an additional devastating loss to the one who is left alone.

5. What is the financial situation? Lack of funds may precipitate a move back to the family. This is difficult for all concerned. Parents, having launched an adult child, feel crowded emotionally and in terms of space; this is especially true if there are grandchildren as well. The parents may find themselves in the role of reluctant live-in sitters. The divorced person feels the embarrassment and the regressive pull of a move back home. "I had to move home after my divorce because I had absolutely no money. I worried a lot about returning to my hometown and living with my demanding mother."

6. Are relations with the ex-spouse awkward? Some divorced persons leave the area because the interaction with the former partner is uncomfortable or seeing him or her with someone else is unbearable. A transfer to a branch office may be requested. A divorced woman hoped that her husband would do just that. She thought that this would make things easier for her and her daughter. However, children find divorce traumatic enough without having their non-custodial parent disappear.

7. Is someone else involved? If the custodial parent marries and moves away with the children, this is an incredible blow to the other parent. Attempts are often made in the divorce settlement to prevent this double loss. A later long-distance move can seriously disrupt previously agreed upon arrangements and good working relationships between ex-spouses. The same themes and behaviors that plagued the family at the time of separation are reignited.[4]

However, long-distance parenting can be rewarding if handled thoughtfully. Isolina Ricci, in her book *Mom's House, Dad's House,* offers practical suggestions for keeping in touch with children across the miles. These include weekly telephone calls; stamped, self-addressed envelopes; cassette tapes for correspondence and bedtime stories; connecting with the child's school; reassuring the child of your love; taking pictures of your life and environment; and a "thinking of you" box filled with small mementos collected between visits.[5]

8. What about jobs? These can have a major influence on moving after a divorce. Those with good positions are reluctant to give them up in order to move. Conversely, a good job opening elsewhere increases motivation to relocate.

Most moves take place soon after separation and before the legal divorce. In one study, 65 percent of those who moved relocated within a month of the separation, and an additional 25 percent moved before the divorce. Forty-eight percent of the movers returned to an area they had previously lived in.[6] Few moves occur after divorce, except in the case of remarriage or a new job opportunity.

Among the more serious problems of moving after a divorce are being too close to one's family, being too far from children, loneliness, financial difficulties, and job related problems.[7] A woman who has "been taken care of" by her husband feels especially overwhelmed when dealing with multiple issues that she hasn't had to cope with before: "I was absolutely paralyzed by landlord problems the first months and felt extremely isolated. I couldn't eat or sleep."

Safety is another important issue for both divorcees and single women when they move. They can feel totally vulnerable, especially if they have been accustomed to living with another person. The cruel telephone call in the middle of the night is a terrifying experience. Living in fear for one's physical well-being creates enormous anxiety and unhappiness. Loneliness is another major factor for both men and women.

Men may have more problems than women with the logistics of settling into a new location. Generally, they are not accustomed to setting up a household and reaching out to make friends—tasks that have previously been taken care of by their wives. However, a single, available male is considered to be more desirable socially and less threatening than is a single female. New acquaintances are apt to include him in their social circles.

Certainly, moves after a divorce can be painful experiences. The time of a divorce, however, is also an opportunity to reevaluate one's life and to make some new beginnings. Ideally, the ultimate outcome is personal growth:

> Other moves helped me to broaden my horizons and to expand outwardly. This last move after my divorce forced me to grow inwardly and to expand my awareness of my own behavior patterns. Some of the puzzle pieces in my personal life have begun to fit together. I discovered who I am sexually and psychologically.

Coping with a Move as a Single

Coping with a move as a single can be difficult. One misses the close working relationship and the intimacy and trust of long-term friends. "I didn't cope well. I spent a lot of time alone—smoked more, drank more. It took me a full year to adjust, and I don't think I ever returned to my former way of functioning."

The move can be especially difficult if unexpected problems arise and there is no one to lean on. One woman reported that a sick dog, a burned out transmission, and an inability to find an apartment almost did her in. Her recommendation is to "be sure to have enough money to cover unexpected expenses."

As with children, extroverted adults make the best adjustment to a move.

> My introspective side doesn't mix with my need to socialize and make new friends. It's counterproductive. I like to think things through and be alone, and yet I know I need to get out and meet people.

Singles may have a particularly difficult time in the new community if they do not have any social contacts. Unlike families, they do not have a built-in support system. Finding friends and keeping them is difficult, especially in urban areas where transiency is prevalent. For example, in San Francisco the average length of stay for a single adult is eighteen months. Many come to this city with high hopes. They do not find the ideal job on which they had their hearts set, expenses are high, and, as with many other cities, it is not easy to break into the social circles. "People come and go in your life when you are single. You can't settle in on a relationship and count on it."

Sometimes the home that they left starts looking pretty good, and they miss the familiar. They find themselves returning home for a "fix" and ending up staying. If they make it in the new community, though the struggles may be painful, with each success comes greater confidence and an increased ability to cope and grow. "I was so proud of myself for conquering Manhattan. The feeling of self-esteem is almost intoxicating!"

Positives in a Move

> Moving is a creative and exciting opportunity if you open yourself to it.

Many of our single respondents listed reasons why they enjoyed their moves: The move allowed them to remain with their friends; to enjoy different cities and jobs; to face a challenge; to give an opportunity for experimentation; to conquer a new place; to experience change; to find freedom, independence, and increased self-worth; to know themselves as unique persons despite the struggle, or maybe because of it; and to interact with many different people.

Some interviewees had suggestions to help make the moves of our single readers successful ones.

—You don't have to do the unpacking all at once. Allow yourself time to have fun.

—Identify what makes "home" a home to you. Maybe it is Indian woven baskets, perhaps an art display, or a cozy corner to read in. Whatever it is, make it part of your new place as soon as possible. It will help you to reestablish roots.

—Join a church with an active singles' group and *get involved.* One respondent said, "One of the biggest pluses of the move is that I've strengthened spiritually and in my relationship with God. In the process, I've learned a lot about who I am and what is important in life."

—Get to know your environment. It is too easy for you to plunge anxiously into your new job. Don't disappear behind a desk. Find out what the community has to offer you.

—Who do you want to meet? Learn where they congregate. There are special interest groups doing just about anything you can think of. Find them! If hiking is your thing, join the Sierra or Rocky Mountain clubs. If you are interested in communication, volunteer at a public broadcasting station. If you love politics, you can always find someone running for something.

—Try out different volunteer groups. If they prove not to be what you want, your time has not been wasted. See it as part of your growth, your expansion of boundaries.

—Above all, don't join something just because singles go there. Imagine yourself hating jogging, but ending up in a marathon! Go because you enjoy the featured activities. At least you will have a good time even if you do not meet anyone special.

Whether a move is made for college, a job, a relationship, or a divorce, this is the chance for each individual to learn more about himself or herself, about new places, and about interesting people. One can celebrate the opportunity and make it a positive experience.

Notes

1. Janet Barkas, *Single in America* (New York: Atheneum Press, 1980), p. 21.

2. Jacob Mincer, "Family Migration Decisions." *Journal of Political Economy* 86 (October 1978):758.

3. Catalyst, *Human Factors in Relocation: Corporate and Employee Points of View*. A research project conducted by Catalyst. Funded by Bekins Van Lines (1983), pp. 34-35.

4. Isolina Ricci, *Mom's House, Dad's House* (New York: Macmillan, 1980), p. 203.

5. Ibid., p. 211.

6. Shirley Asher and Bernard Bloom, "Geographic Mobility as a Factor in Adjustment to Divorce." *Journal of Divorce* 6 (Summer 1983):73.

7. Ibid, p. 75.

CHAPTER 6

Special Situations

In this chapter, we will explore moves that are related to special situations. Included are moves resulting from military duty, assignments abroad, and retirement.

Moving and Military Duty

> A woman married to a man with a military career *knows* that moving is a necessary part of life. We have moving down to a system that works well. In twelve years of marriage I've moved seven times, and I love it!

For the military family, mobility is a way of life, which may or may not be a positive experience. Assignments to a particular station usually last only two or three years although recently, in some areas, this time is being extended to four years in order to save on the military budget. The relocation may be to a military community that is similar to the previous one. In this case, "[It] is intended to replace the grass roots of a hometown and to offer security and stability for parents and children alike."[1] The government can clone this community almost anywhere in the world. However, there are some exceptions to this; R.O.T.C. assignments are located at colleges and universities and virtually every city of any size in the United States. In these instances, you are on your own and the military support system is not there.

Until World War II, there seemed to be little official concern for Army wives. The view was that the wife should never complain when she had to move, and most articles on the topic dealt with etiquette in the military. For example, in *The Army Wife*, Nancy Shea wrote, "It usually takes a few hours, sometimes a few days to adjust oneself to orders that involve a change of station, but *adjust you must.*"[2] That was all she had to say about the emotional reaction to a move. Even today, guide books that are written to help the military wife adapt to her prescribed role indicate that deviation from that role is seen as character weakness in the wife rather than as a problem in the system.[3]

The wives of both enlisted men and officers are increasingly influencing military policy. The major factor in a husband's decision to leave the military or to reenlist is the attitude of his wife. Dissatisfied wives cite frequent relocation and family separation at the time of a move as major problems.[4]

Wives of military men are not the only ones who are concerned about the impact of moving. *The New York Times Magazine,* did a report on 119 women who had entered the United States Military Academy at West Point in 1976. Interviews were conducted five years after their graduation, when these women were having to make career choices about whether to remain in the military. A major factor in the decision to leave was the conflict between military demands, and family needs, specifically in the area of mobility.[5] One lieutenant said that she did not want her children to grow up with the same sense of rootlessness that she felt as a child in a military family.

However, one Navy wife reported that by identifying home as the place where aunts, uncles, grandparents, and cousins lived, their family never felt rootless. They always returned there in the summers and between moves from one duty station to another. To have such a consistent place is viewed by many respondents as important to family stability and continuity.

Although the military requires families to move, the government does not necessarily subsidize all expenses connected with relocation, nor is housing always provided. If there is housing, there is often a wait to get into these quarters, which means one more move. Or it may be that there are no military quarters available at all. For example,

The Pentagon has few military quarters for five thousand officers. The D.C. area is one of the most expensive areas in the United States. To be able to afford to rent, most military personnel live a minimum of an hour's commute from work and all in different directions.

Expenses seem to be a major issue for many families, since money lost is not recoverable. "There is a joke in the Army. What is the first thing you do after you move? Answer: Start saving for the next move! Unfortunately, it can cost you thousands of dollars to move."

In addition, several families mentioned the problem of negotiating with the local school systems, which may be less than cooperative with temporary moves. The quality of education differs greatly among communities across the country, and a required course in one state might not even be accepted in another. A teenager indicated that an additional problem is being located in a base near a wealthy area.

All of us from the base stood out because we didn't wear expensive clothes like the local kids did. It was hard to be accepted. When the ninth grade graduation dance was held, I was one of only two who weren't invited.

However, to show that something good can emerge from something painful, the same person said, "On the next move, I decided that I was going to be part of the 'in' crowd and made it through sheer determination."

Although attempts have been made to make transitions easier, relocation services for the families of military personnel vary a great deal, since base programs are not uniform. The Army Community Service, the Air Force Family Service Programs, and the Navy Family Service Center were established in large part because of relocation problems. Travis Air Force Base in California opened a Family Support Center, which gives "smooth move" seminars to help families and to reduce their stress and uncertainty. Some of these seminars focus only on the logistics of a move, but others are concerned with the family's psychological well-being, also. One respondent noted that the military provides help with a variety of clubs and volunteer organizations. Being able to attend these is one of the pluses of living on the post.

A relatively new (1981) magazine called *Military Family* is now published bimonthly, which suggests that family problems are being taken more seriously. It features articles on military life that deal with domestic violence, child abuse, alcoholism, finances, spouse employment, and relocation. The magazine offers the names of books and workshops that can help those in the military with family problems.

It is interesting to compare military families to corporate families[6] and to find that there are both similarities and differences. Both share certain problems: The husband must move for advancement, but he maintains basic job continuity in the move. There is little choice regarding location. The extended family often lives far away. The wife is expected to be loyal to her husband's commitments. Those who are in the process of getting a degree encounter serious problems in finding suitable schools, in completing requirements, in transferring credits, and in financing education. Career relocation for the wife is difficult, since the couple may be in an area where there is no available employment; an additional problem for the military wife is discrimination by potential employers because of known transiency of the wife. The wife is affected by a loss of benefits from her previous job, difficulty in career continuity, and lack of uniformity in state licensing and certification (consistently, the wives who were interviewed indicated a career loss since they were unable to find work in their fields). Because of the increase of women's influence, in recent years women's feelings about moving have been taken into account in both the corporate and the military worlds. And after the move there is often a financial loss for the family because of the expense of the move and the wife's unemployment.

One respondent indicated that she has never found it difficult to get a job. She feels that too many women are apologetic for the fact that they will be in the community for only three to four years. "We need to emphasize our positive job potential."

There are also differences between military and corporate families. The military wife has advantages not enjoyed by the corporate wife. A major advantage is that she moves into a setting that is, to some extent, familiar. Often everyone else on the post has a similar situation and life-style. Rules of behavior and expectations seldom change from one post to another. Sometimes the family reconnects with former acquaintances whom they had met at other duty stations. This sense of the familiar is not as prevalent in the corporate world.

One respondent indicated that there have been some big changes in the last few years in the military world.

> The "traditional" rules of behavior and expectation have changed radically. Welcoming neighbors with doughnuts and pots of coffee are the exception; membership in the Officers' Wives Club is minimal. Unit level coffee/luncheon groups are few and far between. The clubs and volunteer organizations are there, but the military wife must seek them out.

In the military, the first choice of location occurs with retirement. If one is career military, retirement may take place as early as forty-five years of age. One woman anticipated this kind of youthful retirement eagerly because she and her husband planned to pick a location in which he could get a job and she could finally pursue her own career. Since the wives of military personnel are generally well educated and often frustrated by not having the opportunity to actualize their potential, their husbands' retirement may offer them their first chance to advance in a career and to develop professional status. Wrote one military wife:

> I feel that the most difficult part of the military move for the wife is the necessity of "proving" herself every time she moves. The military man puts his rank on his sleeve or on his shoulder, and everyone knows a great deal about his capabilities, his level of responsibility, and so on. The spouse wears no badge of level of capability. This is especially true for the wife/mother/volunteer. She doesn't even have a resume and must start from scratch with each move.

These words echoed those of a corporate wife, who said that she had headed up the Girl Scout program of her community, but when she moved, she could not even get a slot as a Scout leader.

According to Jerry McKain's research, reaction to a military move depends on how those involved define mobility. Is it viewed as an opportunity or as a threatening experience? What is the attitude toward the community to which one is sent? Is there identification with the military community? What is the family living situation?' The importance of these issues was validated by those whom we interviewed.

McKain also found that the personality attributes of wives are significant. Women who score "high" on alienation and lacked identification with the military felt socially isolated and were open to personal, marital, and family problems. By contrast, a wife who is "low" on alienation seems to take moves in stride and quickly becomes integrated into life at the base. McKain suggested that "sponsors" might be used to help families during the adjustment period. Evidently the Navy has been using the sponsor system since 1970.

What our interviewees found most helpful in moving from one location to another was to learn as much as possible about the places to which they were going in advance and then to explore them with their families. *Get out* is the message.

Life in the military provides a structure and a certain amount of security. These families probably make more moves than any other individual group. One of the potential joys—which is an opportunity for many in the military—is the chance to live abroad and to share that experience with the family.

International Moves

Some families, couples, and single people have the opportunity to live abroad. Most international moves are temporary—generally around three years—although one may move from one overseas spot to another with brief periods of time back in the United States. For these individuals or families, flexibility is important in order to adjust quickly to new cultures and new ways of life.

A single woman who worked for the government reported that she thoroughly enjoyed her time abroad. She was able to have some choice as to where she lived and, at various times, selected France, England, and Japan, among other countries. She felt strongly that it was advantageous to live in the community instead of on the compound. A military couple echoed her view.

> The opportunity to live and work with Germans was really special. We lived in a small village that had a slow pace. The shopkeepers and neighbors were like a second family. The chance to travel throughout Europe was absolute magic and the opportunity of a lifetime.

Another single woman, who worked for the Red Cross, had twenty years of frequent moves and many different cultural experiences. She eventually decided to put down roots and took a more traditional position "stateside." The adjustment to being in one place was considerable, and she missed the excitement of constant change.

People's reasons for living abroad vary. For some, it is an opportunity to "see the world" and to be exposed to other cultures. Others feel a particular geographic pull. A single man was drawn to Third World countries. He associated this desire with his adventuresome grandmother, who traveled alone extensively. He greatly admired her spirit. Missionaries feel called to share their faith. They are frequently assigned to one spot and stay there for the length of their service, learning the language and becoming integral parts of the community. Recently, several mission boards have required that religious enthusiasm be buttressed by secular training in fields such as medicine, agriculture, mechanics, or social services.

Many who go abroad have little choice (which is important for satisfaction) in this decision. The military hierarchy decides when and whether its personnel make an overseas move. A multinational corporation may require those who are moving up the ladder to have overseas experience.

To turn down too many moves is to seal your fate. You need to "get your ticket punched." One difficulty with an overseas move is that there is no guarantee that you will be reassigned to the same city you left, so you won't necessarily go back to where your former friends live.

There are other reasons for concern.

The life for singles may be very lonely. I always thought I was a loner. Living abroad made me realize how much I needed closeness and the quasi-family I had left behind. I learned a lot about myself.

Even daily meals may be a problem because of the uncertainty about language, cultural patterns, and health issues. Shopping and cooking in other countries is a far cry from doing so in the United States. One woman wrote: "A friend of mine who went to Norway spent two months looking for a jar of mayonnaise, only to find that it came in a tube there . . . like toothpaste."

Mealtime is only one of the areas of adjustment.

A wife must transplant family life to different surroundings, build new friendships, adjust to dirt and heat in the home, worry about health and the schools, get used to the invasion of privacy by omnipresent servants, and try to learn a strange tongue in two to three distracted hours a week.[8]

Under these circumstances, distance from family and friends can be overwhelming.

The effect of overseas moves on marriages is mixed. Mutual reliance on each other brought one couple closer than ever before. "In our experience, marriages overseas do not remain in a *status quo*. They either improve or crumble."

One man, working for the State Department, said that his marriage ended because his wife wanted to have the opportunity to pursue her own career. She also longed to put down roots. Another couple was stressed by one-sided dependency after they moved to Japan. The wife leaned on her husband more than either of them were comfortable with because she was unfamiliar with the culture and language. Still another wife reported that a series of overseas moves helped to keep her marriage together temporarily. The excitement and adventure of exploring new horizons served to cover up serious problems, which later erupted in divorce.

Foreign service is usually incompatible with dual career. Some consulates try to create jobs for partners of employees, but these are rarely in the wife's career path. Also, the host countries seldom have positions to offer the working wife. Besides, the wife of an employee is generally expected to entertain and to be available for dinners and receptions. Until recent years, corporation and government wives were graded on the performance of their "duties," although they received no salaries. The conflicting demands of dual careers are becoming increasingly significant in overseas moves. There is concern that, as has happened in the United States, employees will start refusing to transfer abroad.[9]

Most of those with whom we talked believe that children can gain a great deal from living abroad. One respondent indicated that her four young children found this experience an adventure. With multiple moves, their family had lived in thirteen places in fifteen years. However, she believed that when children enter their teens they need more stability—to be in one place for a while—and the chance to develop a network of friends.

Obviously, living abroad is not always easy for children. One young couple indicated that their four-year-old son had a hard time adjusting to Hong Kong. He went to a British school and was labeled a foreigner and laughed at because his pronunciation was different. The parents were unaware of just how difficult it had been for him until they returned to the United States and watched him blossom in school.

Among those who go overseas, about one-third must return home before the contract is completed. Some companies have as high as a 79 percent fall-out rate, and almost all are caused by maladjustment.[10] This figure does not include the individual who suffers from "brown out"—those who remain abroad, but function at a minimal work level.[11] Since the cost of one failure ranges from $80,000 to well over $100,000, the expense to the corporation is enormous. In addition to the dollar cost, there is loss of time and opportunity for the business, loss of reputation to the government or corporation, and a terrible sense of failure experienced by the employee and his or her family.

Some assignments are considered more difficult than are others. India, Pakistan, Southeast Asia, the Middle East, North and East Africa, and Liberia are problem areas for finding job satisfaction, skilled coworkers, housing, health care, entertainment, food, and minimal stress. These are also areas in which the greatest cultural barriers exist. In some of these countries, it is particularly hard for women to adapt because of inherent male dominated value systems.[12] One couple said that Mexico should be added to the list of "difficult" countries in which to live.

A banker indicated that he felt the number of years that a person was assigned abroad needed to vary according to the country—one year in some countries to an almost unlimited number of years in others. From his perspective, the variable depended on the enormity in the gap between the rich and the poor. This discrepancy begins to eat away at one's values and creates a personally damaging internal detachment, which then affects all relationships.

One factor that is repeatedly emphasized in the literature is the importance of adequate training programs before moving. Unfortunately, most people who live in countries that are not native to them have had a minimal amount of preparation. Said one interviewee:

> We were told that the food is great and the people are friendly. When I asked the man who was sharing this information how long ago he had lived in this particular country, he replied, "I've never been there." That was our indoctrination!

Corporations often feel that the stay will be reasonably short (usually three years or less) and, therefore, not worth the expense of the pre-moving training. Also, the time between assignment and leaving is often rather short. Considering the fall-out and brown-out rates, the government and corporations are shortsighted in this matter.

Four important factors need to be considered with regard to overseas moves. These are: assessment of whom to send; predeparture training; on-site support; and reentry counseling. [13]

Assessment of Whom to Send

A person who functions beautifully in his or her native country will not necessarily do well abroad. One cannot rely on home values and behavior patterns. Particular characteristics are necessary, and it is possible for companies to measure these characteristics before assigning employees to overseas service. [14] If you are considering an overseas move, see if you fit this profile.

—The ability to find interests and activities in the new country.
—Low vulnerability to stress, depression, and loneliness.
—Confidence in your expertise and ability to accomplish the prospective job.
—The ability to develop lasting friendships.
—Willingness to use the language of the country, which will facilitate involvement with new friends.
—An appreciative, non-judgmental attitude toward differing beliefs, values, and behaviors.
—Flexibility, patience, and willingness to adapt.

A woman who was described as the "ideal person" was much in demand in the country to which she had been assigned. She treated the natives with respect and valued their ideas. She listened intently, asking appropriate questions. She never "spoke down" to anyone, and she encouraged the use of the local language in training and communication. [15]

Predeparture Training

There are many things that could help in the predeparture training but, unfortunately, most of them are not included in whatever training is available. If there is training, much of it focuses on business matters rather than on cultural issues. Tragedies have occurred because executives, and others, did not understand the unwritten rules of the particular country to which they had been assigned.

Training should be country specific rather than generalized, since there are many differences among nations. Some colleges offer courses in overseas orientation and "culture-grams," complete packages for various countries.[16]

It is important to learn the language in advance, even if most of the population speaks English. Citizens appreciate any attempt to communicate in their native tongue. Even thirty hours of study can give rudiments of the language, and the mover will not feel so totally lost on arrival. Non-verbal language is also an important part of your study. A woman living in India found it hard to remember that shaking one's head side-to-side meant yes, not no.

Other predeparture suggestions for international moves are: see some audio-visual tapes, meet with a returning family for first-hand information (emphasized as particularly important by several interviewees), and become immersed in novels and nonfiction books that can help one understand the cultural heritage, attitudes, customs, and social structure of the country.[17] Obviously, a visit to the new location before moving there would be ideal, but it is not always realistic. One couple we interviewed had just turned down an overseas assignment after visiting the projected host country. They discovered, at a party to which they had been invited, that *nobody* from the corporation liked being there! This couple was fortunate to have had the choice to say no to the move.

One of the major problems with predeparture training programs is that wives and teenaged children are seldom included in them. If family members have the opportunity to be a part of such discussions, areas of concern may be determined in advance.

On-site Support

Once arriving in the new country, even though homework is well done, the mover will have much to learn and many questions to ask. The integration process continues for several months. Having a sponsor with whom to talk can alleviate much anxiety after a move. (Again, this was referred to as most helpful.) One respondent mentioned the American Women's Clubs as being useful in all the countries to which she and her husband went. Indoctrination classes are offered by some churches and other groups in different countries. These are generally held during the day, however, when the working spouse or single person is unable to attend.

Reentry Counseling

Reentry counseling is also important, though it seems to get even less attention than predeparture training. Some of our respondents found that settling back into the United States was tougher than going abroad. The impact is twice as strong because it is often unexpected.

> Returning to Los Angeles from Europe was a culture shock. I had been away for five years and was totally out of touch with the United States. Europe is so private. People live unto themselves. Los Angeles seemed plastic. I felt overwhelmed and wanted to go back to Europe. My sense of confidence was gone. I just insulated myself against everything. It took six months for me to come out of my stunned state.

According to another respondent, reentry is facilitated by coming back to an international city.

Another problem with reentry is that servants often come with the new position in a foreign country. Upon returning to the United States, not only are there no servants, but also the wife and mother often has to go to work to make ends meet. The family discovers, with horror, that housing costs may have doubled in the time since they left. The advice used to be to sell your house and buy another one when you returned from overseas. Evidently, there has been a shift, and those persons who are sent abroad are now advised to hold onto their real estate. "Even if you don't return to the same place, at least you'll have some equity."

Another couple, adjusting to the move back home, reflected on the beautiful simplicity of India—the concrete floors and clay walls and living with basic necessities. They found themselves critical of most Americans' overabundance of material goods.

Not surprisingly, children also go through readjustment problems. A State Department employee reported that his teenaged children were stunned by the lack of awareness of their American peers of world issues. They went out for an evening and came home early. "Cruising" was of no interest to them. They felt as if they had been dropped from another planet.

Although there are certainly mixed reactions to an overseas move, most of the families with whom we had contact viewed their time abroad as a positive experience. One man expressed the feelings of many others.

> Living in Europe was like stepping back into the Middle Ages. At first the strangeness was a little frightening. However, there were many pluses for my wife and me—the incredible scenery, the languages, the architecture, and the people whom we came to know. We would not have wanted to miss any of it.

Moves for Retirement

> I walk through the house, touching, remembering. I catch glimpses of little pink-cheeked sprites. I stare at the house, the yard, the park, trying to etch them forever on my mind. I drive through the city looking at the colleges, the village, familiar houses. I weep for my loss.

For most people, anticipation of retirement is underway well before the retirement date.[18] The mind and heart start preparing for that moment about fifteen years in advance. Some people take a more active role than others in getting ready for retirement, but even those who are indifferent to that stage of life, or who dread it and try to pretend it will never come, have thoughts of retirement in the back of their minds. As the time draws closer, in the late fifties and early sixties, involvement in the process escalates and decisions around when and where to retire are made and remade.

Attitudes toward retirement vary greatly. Those who project new careers often choose early retirement. They enjoy their current work, but feel it lacks meaning or has become too all-consuming.[19] Some anticipate developing a neglected part of themselves, such as an artistic talent, or they see retirement as a stepping stone to exciting opportunities. They look forward to the chance to function as consultants, to write, or to take some other direction in their field or perhaps in a new one. This "new direction" may or may not provide monetary rewards.

Optional, paid employment opportunities have a demonstrably positive effect on the well-being of some retirees,[20] but people who have little time for social activities in their preretirement years are often eager for the freedom of retirement without structure. As one respondent reported, "To have the luxury of free time can be a great gift." However, they may overestimate the joy of having an abundance of leisure time and become disillusioned and bored.

Workaholics, who view productivity as their only meaningful participation in life, dread retirement because they know it will leave a gap in their lives. Caught up in the work ethic, they see themselves as a potential burden on their families and on society unless they are wise enough to become involved before retirement in self-directed projects or in favorite voluntary causes.

Retirement Planning

Some form of retirement counseling or planning is helpful for most people. Just as anticipatory socialization is required before entering the world of work, so also it is important as one looks toward retirement.[21]

A few corporations and professional groups offer retirement seminars. The benefits of such preretirement planning sessions depend on their format and content. One author suggests a human potential model as the most effective approach. This combines behavioral change (building on one's strengths, accomplishments, and successes); practical tips; individual and small group discussions on relevant topics; and an opportunity to explore the emotional aspects of approaching retirement.[22] Such seminars are conducted with a positive view of retirement. Those who attend come away seeing retirement as an active, rather than a passive, context; they view it as a life-stage they can direct instead of something over which they have no control.

One question brought up in seminars is "Where will I live?" The response to this question depends on answers to many other questions: "When will I retire?" "What is the state of my finances?" "How is my health?" (The last two questions are probably the most important determining factors.) "Where do my children live?" "Where are my friends?" Married partners need equal input. We will look at each of these factors that affect decisions about moving.

Key Decisions

The *when* of retirement was not an issue in the early part of this century, since most people died while still employed. Now, however, one-quarter of our lives may come after we reach the age of sixty-five. For a while, early retirement was touted as the way to go, but in recent years that trend seems to be reversing itself.[23] Still, companies that move, consolidate, merge, or want to lower overhead costs offer early retirement, which accelerates the time frame compared to the usual retirement considerations.

The question of *where* you will live occupies much time and discussion. Although about 25 percent of those who retire leave their positions for health reasons,[24] the majority of retirees are in good health and intend to stay that way. Their choice of location is strongly influenced by the presence of good hospitals and medical facilities. Also, they view adequate transportation as important for the years when they will no longer be able to drive.

Finances are a crucial consideration. An article in *Time* magazine indicated that the American population is getting older and that the elderly now have more money than ever before.[25] A rule of thumb for planning for a satisfactory income in retirement is 60 to 70 percent of one's preretirement salary. Many people want to work until their pension plan allows for such coverage. This amount generally makes it possible to continue living reasonably close to the style to which one has become accustomed. The thought of not having enough money is frightening. There are so many stories of elderly persons living in tiny flats, barely able to survive, that this concern is very much a part of our conscious awareness.

Family and friends are another important part of the decision making process. Many move in order to be closer to their children and grandchildren, even if that means leaving a community in which they have spent most of their lives. One woman said, "The move completed our family oneness since we are all together now." The obvious disadvantage of such a plan is that if their children move to another community in order to achieve their own financial and personal goals, then retirees are left facing another move or continuing to live in areas they might not have otherwise selected.

Sometimes retirees must move in with relatives because they do not have enough money to live alone. Depending on the situation, this can be a positive or a negative experience. One respondent indicated that she tries "very hard to be useful," a rather poignant comment. Ground rules and a structure need to be laid down ahead of time for the protection of both the retiree and the host family. A couple of families with whom we spoke had done some creative thinking on this issue. In a dual career family, having a parent available for the children can be a real blessing. If the parent is paid a salary as a day care person, both generations feel a certain freedom with regard to expectations.

Climate is a strong determinant of where to live. Movers go to the Sunbelt areas of Florida, California, Arizona, New

Mexico, and Texas. They are usually leaving Northern and Northeastern states. Even if they don't move away from their primary residences, many retirees go to these warmer areas in the winter, either renting a home, having a second home, or joining hundreds of others in motor home villages. Groups of friends may travel in caravans to these locations, providing familiar company for the winter months.

Age Segregated Communities

One popular choice for living after retirement is segregated residences. Many thousands of retirees sell their homes and leave apartments to move into such communities. For some popular ones, application must be made six to ten years in advance.

Some of these are expensive life-care facilities and, therefore, are not affordable to many who retire. However, one of our interviewees had entered a H.U.D. financed retirement high rise. Thirty percent of her income was used to pay the rent. This percentage is the same no matter how much or how little income one has.

Living in a retirement complex provides safety and predictability. Well-balanced meals help to maintain health; the fellowship, which might be lacking in an apartment or home, prevents isolation. One man said: "We have made many more friends here than we had in Florida, where we lived for many years. You don't expect to make good friends at this time of your life."

In addition to the above advantages, there is much comfort in knowing that, faced with one's own illness or a partner's death, a support system is immediately available. Those who choose to live in retirement facilities generally either have no close relatives or they do not want to be dependent on their children or other relatives as they grow older. Also, they wish to make their own decisions as to where to spend the rest of their lives.

Some retirement homes offer the opportunity for the prospective resident to try them out before selling his or her home and moving in. This is a wise idea even if the retirement facility is in your own town or city. One woman with whom we talked said that several couples she knew urged her to move into their retirement home. She did so on a temporary basis. After a week, she decided that this option was not the best for her, and she kept her home. One interviewee, who is from a retirement center, said that the residents can form strong cliques and that newcomers may have trouble breaking in—another good reason to try out a place in advance.

It is important to take time before making a decision. A retired woman moved into a residence that did not offer life care and, later, wondered if that was the best choice. It is equally important that contracts be read carefully so that it is clear what services are being offered and there are no unpleasant surprises.

The American Association of Retired Persons gives information about retirement facilities all over the country. In fact an interviewee proclaimed A.A.R.P. membership as the "biggest bargain available" because of all the many benefits the organization offers.

Making the Decision Whether to Move

Satisfaction with retirement choices is remarkably high. Over 70 percent of those polled in one study indicated that they viewed retirement as basically good.[26] Those who were not happy had less autonomy in making their choices as to where to live. They have rented rather than owned their preretirement homes. Their financial and occupational status is low. Their health is poor. They did not prepare themselves for retirement. And they did not move into friendly, supportive communities.[27]

Some retirees seem to have a low overall interest in moving at all. Generally those who prefer their current location are widowed, divorced, or have many friends or family nearby. They also may intend to continue to be active in their professional groups.

In what concrete ways can you determine whether or not

(and where) to move? It will probably be the first time that moving for a job is not a major consideration. If your business takes you on trips around the country, you have the opportunity to start looking for places you might consider desirable long before retirement.

One process for making a decision is as follows:
—Use the decision making instrument in the second chapter, which indicates what is most important to you.
—Compare these with your partner if you are making the move with someone else.
—Compile a joint list.
—Which of the several communities you are considering would accommodate these needs.? If you don't have enough information on a particular location, do some research and find out as much as you can about the communities of choice.

One couple for whom this process worked well described the results.

> We both felt that cultural opportunities were important, as were excellent health services and lack of snow. Also, we wanted to stay with our professional activities as much as possible. However, most of our close friends still lived in the semi-rural community from which we had moved ten years earlier. We decided to stay where we were, but allowed for visits to our former community, staying at an inexpensive bed and breakfast. This way we felt that we could balance the best of both worlds. We can still shift our location if we want to after trying this for awhile.

Another suggestion regarding choosing a place to live is offered by Human Habitat Research, which promises to help people find "the perfect place to live" according to their needs and desires. This company produces a list of twenty recommended locations from a selection of sixteen thousand cities and towns in the United States. Their recommendations are based on respondents' answers to one hundred questions from a Personal Preference Selection Guide.[28]

If you move, you will generally have a deep sense of loss at leaving your familiar home. This is especially true if you have lived there a long time or are moving alone because of a death or divorce. Many memories may flood your mind and emotions.

> Another part of my distress is a realization that the first two parts of my life are over: growing up, which involved schooling and starting work; and marriage, having children, and advancement in my career. Sometimes I find myself sadly realizing that I'll never again be in "my home" with two little tow-headed kids running around. It's not that I really want to go back and relive those years. And yet, if a time machine were available I would hop in it for an occasional afternoon.

What is the adjustment period like for those who relocate after retirement? There are two major time periods. First, there is an initial stressful period of the actual move and developing habitual life patterns in a new location. The second period is a time of developing a sense of long-term satisfaction (or dissatisfaction) in the move.[29] Most people indicated that it takes six to eighteen months to adjust to a retirement move. A few felt that it took much longer to get accustomed to the changes. One respondent wrote: "The time required to make an adjustment depends on the planning and mental preparation for that part of your life. The more convinced you are that this is the best move, the more rapid will be the adjustment."

If you are dissatisfied with a retirement choice, it is important for you to reevaluate and to consider yet one more move. A couple who had lived for many years in Colorado decided, upon retirement, to move near their son in California. Six months later, they were back in Colorado— much to the joy of their friends. The move to California had turned out badly. They were able to acknowledge this and to do something about it. Realizing that you were wrong is far less painful than living out a mistake.

Notes

1. Elizabeth Finlayson, "A Study of the Wife of the Army Officer." In *Families in the Military System,* eds. H. McCubbin et al. (London: Sage Publications, 1976),p. 19.

2. Nancy Shea, *The Army Wife* (New York: Harper, 1941), p. 209.

3. Ellwyn Stoddard, "Changing Spouse Roles: An Analytical Commentary." In *Military Families: Adaptation to Change,* eds. E. Hunter and S. Nice (New York: Praeger, 1978), p. 162.

4. Donald Lund, "Junior Officer Retention in the Modern Voluntary Army." In *Military Families: Adaptation to Change,* eds. E. Hunter and S. Nice (New York: Praeger, 1978),p. 38.

5. E. Fein, "The Choice: Women Officers Decide to Stay in or Leave." *New York Times* Magazine (May 5, 1985):32ff.

6. Janice Rienerth, "Separations and Female Centeredness in the Military Family." In *Military Families: Adaptation to Change,* eds. E. Hunter and S. Nice (New York: Praeger, 1978),p. 172.

7. Jerry McKain, "Relocation in the Military: Alienation and Family Problems." *Journal of Marriage and the Family* 35 (May 1973):209.

8. Afzalur Rahim, "A Model for Developing Key Expatriate Executives." *Personnel Journal* (April 1983):312.

9. Frances Burwell, "Spouse Employment: Much Concern, but Little Consensus." *Foreign Service Journal* 63 (January, 1986):31.

10. Alison Lanier, "Selecting and Preparing Personnel for Overseas Transfers." *Personnel Journal* 58 (March 1979):160.

11. Michael Q. Harvey, "The Multinational Corporations Expatriate Problem: An Application of Murphy's Law." *Business Horizons* 26 (January-February 1983):72.

12. Mark Mendenhall and Gary Oddon, "The Dimensions of Expatriate Acculturation: A Review." *Academy of Management Review* 10 (January 1985): 43.

13. Phillip Harris, "Employees Abroad: Maintain the Corporate Connection." *Personnel Journal* 65 (August 1986):108.

14. Mendenhall and Odden, "The Dimensions of Expatriate Acculturation," p. 40.

15. James McCaffrey and Craig Hafner, "When Two Cultures Collide: Doing Business Overseas." *Training and Development Journal* 39 (October 1985):31.

16. Geraldine Spruell, "How Do You Ensure Success of Managers Going Abroad?" *Training and Development Journal* 39 (December 1985):24.

17. Harvey, "The Multinational Corporations Expatriate Problem: An Application of Murphy's Law," p. 77.

18. Linda Evans, David Ekerdt, and Raymond Bosse, "Proximity to Retirement and Anticipatory Involvement." *Journal of Gerontology* 40 (March 1985):368.

19. Keith Kilty and John Behlina, "Predicting the Retirement Intentions and Attitudes of Professional Workers." *Journal of Gerontology* 40 (February 1985):226.

20. Stephen Soumerai and Jerry Avorn, "Perceived Health, Life Satisfaction, and Activity in the Urban Elderly: A Controlled Study of the Impact of Part-Time Work." *Journal of Gerontology* 38 (March 1983):360.

21. Anita Kamoun and John Cavanaugh, "The Impact of Preretirement Education Programmes on Workers Preretirement Socialization." *Journal of Occupational Behavior* 7 (July 1986):245.

22. Jeffrey Giordano and Nan Hervig Giordano, "A Classification of Preretirement Programs: In Search of a New Model." *Educational Gerontology* 9 (March-June1983):130.

23. David Ekerdt, Raymond Bosse, and Robert Glynn, "Period Effects on Planned Age for Retirement." *Research on Aging* 7 (September 1985):404.

24. Clyde Hendrick, Karen Wells, and Martin Faletti, "Social and Emotional Effects of Geographic Relocation on Elderly Retirees." *Journal of Personality and Social Psychology* 42 (May 1982):954.

25. Jon D. Hull, "Insurance for the Twilight Years." *Time* (April 6, 1987): 53.

26. Hendrick, Wells, Faletti, "Social and Emotional Effects of Geographic Relocation on Elderly Retirees," p. 961.

27. Ibid, p. 958.

28. "Utopia by Computer." *Harper's* 275 (September 1987):28.

29. Hendrick, Wells, Faletti, "Social and Emotional Effects of Geographic Relocation on Elderly Retirees," p. 951.

PART III

The Process of Moving:
Practical and Psychological
Issues

CHAPTER 7

Practical Tips for Moving

In part 2 we wrote about the people we interviewed and their experiences. In part 3, we write to you, the reader, with concrete suggestions that will help you with this and future moves.

Moving day is not just twenty-four hours; it is a process, beginning with the decision to relocate and ending when you are unpacked and have found the doctors, schools, services, and shops that allow you to feel reasonably safe and sorted out in your new setting. Whether you feel competent in the situation or out of control depends a great deal on your attitude. Unhappy movers often feel overwhelmed from start to finish.

> Moving Day is that sinking feeling in my stomach when we first consider relocation. It is dreams of being caught in an avalanche of packing cases. It is the day itself—so long and strenuous that I wonder how I can see it through. It is finding, weeks later, still another box that must be emptied.

Movers who are utterly discouraged tend to react rather than act in their situations. They feel helpless to influence what is happening to them and scarcely prepare for the multitude of decisions and activities involved in relocation. In contrast, preplanning is the key for satisfied movers who feel competent and in charge of their move. Learning to handle the practical problems of moving is seen by them as part of their overall adjustment to relocation. They are challenged to cope with the external and objective aspects of moving (discussed in this chapter) as well as with the internal and subjective aspects (discussed in the next chapter).

This chapter is divided into three sections, which deal, in turn, with advance planning, moving out of your old home, and settling into the new one. The success of a move depends far more on what happens in advance of relocation than on any other time period. It is during these preliminary weeks that you establish your priorities, make decisions, start preparations, attack problems, hone your coping mechanisms, and determine your attitude toward relocation. This period is the foundation for a satisfying move.

As you read the next few pages, some suggestions will be far more meaningful to you than others. Some will be impossible for you in terms of time, situation, or money. We therefore invite you to interact with our proposals. Bring your own ingenuity into play when an appealing idea seems out of reach. Instead of taking a three-day car trip, exploring your new environs after a move, you may need to make expeditions closer to home—such as half-day hikes with sandwiches in a backpack. Try to focus on the goal behind each suggestion—such as becoming comfortable in your new surroundings—and discover the means by which you can reach that goal.

Advance Preparation for Moving

Who Will Move You?

> We moved our first home in the back of our car and the second in a borrowed pickup truck. Next, our furnishings were added to someone else's unfilled van. Later still, we had half a van, and finally we've needed whole vans that are increasingly larger.

The size of the vehicle used to transport your goods is a measure of your increasing possessions as well as of your status. Usually only your early moves are handled entirely by you. As time goes on, you will need help. A major decision, therefore, that governs all your preparations is deciding how much professional help you are willing to pay for. Cost is a more powerful determinant than preference. A do-it-yourself move is obviously more strenuous than having a van line completely pack, move, and unpack you, but it is far less costly. Unless a corporation is arranging your move, you will probably do at least some of the work yourself. Either way, you must *make arrangements at least a month or two in advance* to get the vehicle and the equipment you will need. Remember that you will have more choice of times if you can avoid peak periods, which are June to September, end-of-months, and weekends; you might even get a cut rate if you choose a slack period. (A wide range of moving options is listed in the second part of this chapter, "Moving Out." You will want to consult it and come to a decision well in advance of a move.)

Sort, Toss, or Clean in Your Current Home

One of the satisfactions of packing is the knowledge that you have reduced a mountain of belongings to a large hill. Give yourself a fresh start. Move only essential furnishings because every pound is paid for in personal effort, in money, or in both. Heavy items (such as a well used sofa) may be cheaper to replace than to transport. Try to take nothing soiled or damaged to your new home; clean and repair needed items in advance. You do not want to bring grungy things (or more work for yourself) into a new home.

Treat the belongings of your spouse and children with respect. Remember that one person's junk is another's treasure. A mother later regretted tossing out a dingy felt horse, because her small daughter mourned it for months. A couple gave away the family dog because of complicated pet regulations in the new state and because the dog would have had to be shipped by air. They didn't anticipate the terrible loss to their children. Ask your children to sort out the toys they can no longer use so that another little girl or boy might enjoy them. A child can go with you to take these to Goodwill or the Salvation Army, and be sure to tell the person in charge that they are gifts from the child. Your children may want to leave special toys with friends, and these can be part of their farewells. Never push children to give up items that still hold meaning for them; there are enough other losses to cope with at this time. When thinning out someone else's closet, set aside the items that you would like to discard and check with the owner about throwing them out. Family members will probably be reasonable, and they may even find other items to give away.

Another alternative is to start with a well planned garage sale to garner both fun and money. You can put your children in charge after you have advertized and planned it. Give them 25 percent of the earnings—to be saved for fun during the move; of course, they should get 100 percent for items that they contribute, a prospect that will send them scurrying to clean out drawers and closets. You will find that your children's friends will gather around and eventually bring their parents to your sale.

If the idea of organizing and running a garage sale leaves you cold, but you have some things that would be appropriate for such an event, search the local newspaper ads for someone who does garage sales for a career. Since garage sales have become so popular, some enterprising individuals have begun advertising their services to do all the work and leave you with a good piece of the profits. Whichever way you do it, take any unsold items to Goodwill or the Salvation Army. Your donation is tax deductible.

Preparing the New Home for Your Arrival

Make sure that your new home is in the best possible condition that time and money allow *before* you move into it. You will probably have to go there ahead of time to make certain that it is freshly cleaned or painted and that any additional work has been done. Buy or build those extra kitchen cupboards, and have uncarpeted floors sanded and refinished before you move in. Also, this is the best time to replace deteriorating carpeting. Too often homeowners put up with shabby carpeting for several years, only to find—when they move once more—that they must replace it for the next owner before the house will sell. You might as well enjoy such improvements yourself if you can afford them. A loan for improvements can be added to the house payments.

If you cannot make all the changes you would like to make before moving, floors should take priority. They are much easier to work on if the house is empty of furniture. In any case, on move-in day, protect your floors from grit, soil, and scuffing with sheets of sturdy plastic.

Planning Furniture Arrangement

You can save yourself considerable hassle on moving day by planning the arrangement of furnishings for your new home. The first step is to go through your current home, room by room, and list all the furnishings—something that you should do anyway in case of theft or fire. Your child might enjoy calling out items for you to write down. Try to decide which furnishings to use in the various rooms of your new home. Sell or give away what you do not want to keep.

The second step is to make a scale drawing of each room on graph paper. Be sure to include the size and location of windows and doors, noting the direction that the doors open, since this will effect the placement of furniture and pictures. If you enjoy decorating, make scale models of the furniture you want in each room. You can switch furniture around on your floor plan to your heart's content without straining a single muscle—a homeowner's dream. When you find the best arrangement, tape your tiny furnishings in place, ready to help you on moving day.

Your children can plan the layout of their own rooms with your aid; this will help them feel that they belong in their new environment. Be ready to explain why they cannot shove a bed against a wall where the closet door opens. If there is wallpapering to do, give even preschoolers a choice of a couple of alternative styles of paper, either of which would be acceptable to you.

A third step goes well beyond the furniture arrangement. It involves the measurement of all storage areas. If you record the size and number of shelves in kitchen cupboards, you will be able to decide where dishes, glasses, and pots and pans will fit. You can even plan utility drawers. You will know what can go in each closet if you measure its shelvings, racks, and rods. A friend of ours, who has become an extremely efficient mover, puts fresh shelf-paper in every area. She knows exactly where every personal and house-hold item will go. She makes sure that her new home is completely cleaned, painted, and draped. She is able to unpack and put away everything in two days. She uses unpressured time to plan in advance and, consequently, is able to enjoy her new home immediately. Her attitude is like that of another good mover, who said: "A periodic move is really great. I get rid of so much stuff that we don't need, and the rest is sorted and cleaned. I've loved moving because it's so satisfying to have a fresh beginning."

Preparing Children for the Move

In so far as it is possible, your children need to know that the people and things they love will go with them or will be accessible to them. Wise advice is for parents to ease the transition for small children by having special things available. Ask your children for their favorite food (bubble-gum ice cream?), color (blue?), fictional character (Snoopy?), book, game, toy, and clothing. Take along what you can in an inexpensive, brightly colored satchel for each child. Try to find other high priority items en route to your new home or after arrival. Also, friends won't seem so far away if your children have small address books and writing paper. Preschoolers can dictate their letters for Mom and Dad to write; they can include a picture of themselves standing in front of their new home. One respondent suggested rewarding small ones with a new sticker for their sticker books every hour while in transit; it helps the time to pass.

As noted in chapter 4, the concerns and losses of children—and their fantasies of their new life—should be openly discussed from the time relocation is first planned. They need to be assured that they are an important part of the move, that they can help you, and that you will consider their needs. Talking and working together can draw your family closer than ever.

Planning Your Entry into Your New Community

By looking through your family appointment books, you can make a fairly complete list of the services, shopping, recreational activities, and special interests that are important to family members. Sharing this list with them can help you correct and expand the list. It also allows the family members to tap into important priorities and to determine what they hope to find in their new community. A single woman said that finding doctors and dentists is a real drag, but locating familiar department stores and fast food chains gives a sense of comfort.

Your list may be similar to the one below.

Services

Medical:	doctor (including specialists), pharmacist, dentist (including orthodontist)
Grooming:	barbershop and beauticians, laundry and dry cleaners, health spa, gym
Pets:	veterinarian
Household:	cleaning help, rug cleaner, plumber, utilities (gas, electricity, water, trash), appliances
Outdoors:	gardener, pool service (if you happen to have a pool)
Automobile:	gas station, car wash, service station

Shopping

Food:	supermarket, specialty stores
Clothing:	department store, discount store, fabrics, men's, women's, and children's specialty shops
Household:	hardware, furniture store, appliances

Activities

Sports:	spectator sports—football, baseball, hockey participation sports—find out how to become involved and keep up with your favorites
Lessons:	music, ballet, crafts, tennis, swimming
Outings:	drama, opera, museums, concerts, movies, parks, shopping centers, hobby shops, exhibits, restaurants of various kinds (keep a set of file cards on

	the ones you really like; this is handy when friends come to visit), picnic grounds
Clubs:	recreational, educational, political, social
Religion:	neighborhood church, synagogue

Availability of these activities and interests can be checked out in advance and plans made so that there is something special to look forward to. Several of the people we talked to strongly advised the movers to get a six-week subscription to a newspaper from the city or town to which you will be moving. Doing so will make you familiar with much useful information, such as the civic issues, people, places, stores, and activities that are important there. Also, be sure to contact the water department, utilities, telephone company, and post office well in advance of moving day.

Moving Out

The Range of Alternatives

To move or to be moved—that is the question. The answer rests primarily on balancing cost against physical effort. Relying on a good van line minimizes your decisions, planning, and worry. On the other hand, do-it-yourself moving gives you the incentive to sort out your priorities and your household well in advance. The list below covers the full range of possibilities between a full-service move by a van line and moving yourself. The alternatives range from (1) minimum effort and maximum cost to (8) maximum effort and minimum cost.

1. Complete van line services: Packing, moving, unpacking; putting everything in closets and drawers; arranging for third party housecleaning and servicing of appliances.

2. Van line packs, loads, moves, unloads, and unpacks everything.

3. Van line loads, moves, and unloads; you pack and unpack.

4. Van line moves only heavy items; lightweight items are moved by you. This choice may be especially useful in local moves.

5. Hire two or three young men to move major items. You supervise and help as necessary. (Apparently, only 21 percent of persons who move use a moving company.)

6. Rent a van to move yourself; you do all the packing, unpacking, lifting, and loading. Some companies offer a full choice of aids. You can purchase boxes, tape, and wrapping materials from them. You can rent optional equipment, such as furniture pads, a handtruck, and even a tow bar to pull your car behind the van as well.

7. Rent a van (as in option 6), but improvise, finding your own boxes, and so on. Purchasing or renting needed items saves you time and energy, but it adds to the costs.

8. Use your own truck (or borrow one) to move your household in stages. If the new home is not far away or if you are making frequent trips to work on it, this kind of move may be feasible, but it is a strenuous option. (This is a choice of 55 percent of people who move.)

When a Van Line Moves You

If you decide to hire a moving company, check out the reputation of several van lines before selecting one. Your city librarian can help you find ratings, and acquaintances who have recently moved can recommend that you use or avoid the company that moved them. The cost of moving is determined by (1) the net weight of your goods (a full van less empty van weight), (2) the distance to be traveled, and (3) the number of hours the employees of the moving company will work. Get two or three estimates and a full written statement of expenses in advance. You still have to pay by weight, but if the company refuses to give you an estimate, look somewhere else.

Who will do the moving? Van lines that use untrained workers may cost you less initially, but your belongings may suffer more damage. Ask for a guaranteed moving date in writing. Overbooking is sometimes a problem, and unexpectedly sitting in a half-packed house a couple of extra days is a poor way to start a move.

Your van line will pack everything that you do not specifically exempt. (Two of our respondents stressed that garbage and discards must be put outside the house or you'll find them neatly boxed in your new home.) Make sure that all boxes are marked or color coded for the specific room they are to go into and that items needed on arrival (such as the vacuum cleaner, pots and pans, and a hammer) will be first off the van. Then sit back and watch other people work. If you plan to handle some of these moving tasks yourself, however, you will find helpful tips in the following sections.

When You Move Yourself

If you rent a van to move yourself, there are guidelines to follow. For example, Ryder recommends its twelve foot parcel vans for two roomloads of furniture; its twenty-two foot van holds seven or more roomloads, and there are other sizes in between. Again, make arrangements weeks in advance.

Do-it-yourself movers must start packing well ahead of time. Out of season clothes and equipment are good candidates for packing in advance (you won't need parkas and snowshoes in August) as are holiday items, such as Christmas decorations. With only a few weeks left before moving, you may not have time for certain hobbies, sports, crafts, or entertaining; this equipment can be packed early. Use a colorful marking pen, clearly noting three items of information on each box: a number (starting with 1), contents, and location in the new house (e.g., family room). One of our interviewees emphasized that numbered boxes are really helpful at your new home because you know that the highest numbers were packed last and will be needed first. Numbers also enable you to see that everything arrived.

Find one place in your house where packing boxes can wait for moving day. Stacked up, they are a sign of accomplishment; scattered, they take over your home. If you will be lifting and loading everything, avoid large, unwieldy boxes. Use small boxes for heavy items, packing books flat, but standing china plates and records on their edges, carefully cushioned. Larger, flat, fragile items—such as mirrors and pictures—must be well wrapped. They must also be placed on edge. With mattresses and removable tabletops, position is optional. When you take apart bed frames or desks, strap the parts together and tape to them a small plastic bag containing the nuts and bolts. Good wood furniture is often awkward in shape and is, therefore, more likely to suffer disastrous scratching. Carefully wrap any parts that could be damaged. The day before you leave, disconnect and clean appliances, electrical equipment, stereos, VCRs, and so on, securing all loose parts.

On moving day you must have a do-it-yourself *with help* attitude. You'll need all the relatives and friends that you can gather. For people who have not been filling boxes for weeks, being on the lift and load crew can be rather enjoyable. Large, heavy items are loaded first (using a handtruck), so be sure that no one has a back problem and that everyone is familiar with proper lifting techniques. If you have enough helpers, you'll be orchestrating a caravan from house to van, so carefully plan where various items should go. Have lots of donuts and coffee available and send out for tasty pizza at lunchtime; this is the time for a real break and a chance to chat with these very special people. The rest of the loading will go fairly quickly after the heaviest work is done. (Food and drinks may also be appreciated by professional movers.)

Whether you move yourself or get professional help (or some of both), your house will need to be cleaned after the van is loaded. If your helpers are still eager, they can do it quickly with you. Better still, hire a cleaning crew—fast and thorough—and ask a loyal friend to supervise them after your departure.

Children and Moving Day

One parent facetiously suggested that "moving day would be easier if you put your children in a box and leave the box behind." Most of us can remember the growing irritation evoked by children who were in four inconvenient places at once—jumping off packing cases, in every doorway, on the stairway, and climbing around in the van. They can also ask a steady stream of questions of the men carrying your antique vases. But the only question they ask you is apt to be, "What can I have to eat? I'm hungry."

This unhappy state of affairs need not exist for parents who are aware of what moving—and moving day—means to their children. The exasperating activities described above stem from the excitement and anxiety about the move, their unfamiliarity with the loading procedure, and their own frustrated desire to be part of the action. Moving day will be more satisfying to everyone if the children are given preliminary explanations, "important" tasks to do (such as packing their own toys), and a window from which they can van watch. A short rehearsal of problem issues can be preventive; for example, have a child try to carry a heavy footstool through the doorway that Dad is blocking. Saying "I'm hungry" may be a legitimate reaction to all the excitement. Small packets of snacks should be available. This is not the day to worry about spoiling dinnertime appetites.

Returning to the facetious remark above, you may be astonished to know that children occasionally do get the idea that moving is for the parents only and that they will be left behind. You can imagine the resultant fears of abandonment! Children do not always tell you what is on their minds, so full communication, which includes even toddlers, is essential throughout the relocation process.

Moving In

Our student days were over, and my husband had accepted his first job. We arrived on the twentieth of August with only twelve dollars to our name. We had to borrow ahead on my husband's salary to pay moving costs and to purchase groceries. It was scary to start our new life in debt to the boss, but exciting to know that we were on our way.

Finances

Transferring financial accounts—checking, savings, and securities—takes time and can leave you without access to money and credit in the interim. Establish yourself financially in the new community before closing out your old accounts. If you choose a branch of the same bank, savings and loan institution, or brokerage firm, your record of financial stability will transfer along with your assets.

It is especially important to be solvent during the first few days after a move. You may need to take out some of your savings or a loan (before or after relocating) to get you comfortably through. Take along traveler's checks for ready cash. With a multitude of unexpected expenses popping up, this is not the time to be short of money.

Making Yourself at Home

Unless you have luxury arrangements, your van line will leave you standing among a houseful of furnishings and boxes. You will find that marking a destination on each item has paid off; most of your belongings are in the right room, waiting for you to release their contents. If yours was a do-it-yourself move, the situation will be similar, but you will be exhausted instead of weary. However, if you taped your carefully made floor plan inside each room, the couches, table, chairs, bureaus, and beds are already in place. That's a hopeful beginning. Live with these arrangements for a few weeks to see how they feel. (Remember that when you worked them out you were probably feeling less scattered than you are now.) Advance planning has saved you a lot of pushing and lifting on a strenuous day.

You have several options of what you may do in the days that lie ahead. It is up to you to decide which one, or combination, will be your choice. Below, you have the ABCs of various approaches to unpacking.

—Aggressive: Work frantically for the next few days to get everything unpacked and in place as quickly as possible.

—Burnt Out: Stare at the boxes in discouraged resentment. Depression will rapidly build until you can get some help.

—Casual: Store less urgent boxes, pulling them out only as they are needed. Do the others gradually; you are willing to live with some chaos.

—Delegating: You do not take on the big job of unpacking alone. Have each family member responsible for his or her belongings and for helping with certain other tasks.

—Enthusiastic: Enjoy making a "home" in your new setting. Take time to savor your belongings as you unpack them; they hold beauty and meaning for you and your family.

—Functional: First unpack those items needed for cooking, cleaning, eating, bathing, dressing, playing (let's not forget some fun). Empty only one box at a time, piling up the others in a logical way until you can get to them.

—Get-away: This attractive approach is discussed in the following paragraph.

Be Good to Yourself

A brief vacation at this time can be a way of taking care of yourself. You can take one on the way to your new home, a couple of days after your arrival at the new home, or after you have spent several strenuous days unpacking. If you have a family, your mini-vacation can be an affirmation of your life together and of the importance of each family member. If you are single, treat yourself to a vacation either alone or with a good friend. A man who made a "first job after college" move from coast to coast described a wonderful two-week trip with three close college friends. If you choose to take your break before all the work is done, the furniture and boxes will not unpack themselves in your absence, but you will come back to them refreshed. You have many tomorrows to make your new living quarters into a home.

Note

Some of the ideas in this chapter came from the following sources: Bekins and Connections Relocation Company, 1984. *Connections for Lifestyle Relocation* (LaGrange, Ill.: Connections Relocation Company, 1984); Mayflower Transit, *The Mayflower Moving Kit* (Indianapolis: Aero Mayflower Transit, 1987); Ryder, *The Ryder Mover's Guide* (Miami, Fla.: Ryder Truck Rental, 1985).

CHAPTER 8

Stress and Coping

> *To me, all moves are opportunities. Change is not distress. I've always looked forward to new adventures—learning how to conquer New York City, soaking in Boston's history.*

Some of those persons with whom we talked were enthusiastic about moving. Others had had some difficult periods, but eventually adjusted. Still others continued to be depressed many months after relocating. Why are some people devastated by moves that others enjoy or take in stride?

Occasionally, we interviewed people who had basically the same reactions to any and all moves. "I always love the challenge of new places," or "I've never had a happy move." More often, however, persons who shared their experiences with us identified a range of reactions during their lives; despair characterized one move, indifference a second, and enthusiasm a third.

In this chapter, we will discuss two key influences that make an impact on the success of a particular move. We believe that this information will help you to make a good adjustment to your move.

The two key influences are: (1) The amount of psychological stress involved in the move, and (2) the ways we use particular coping mechanisms to deal with this stress. We will look at stress and coping in turn. This is a somewhat more technical part of our book, but it can be very useful to you in understanding your responses to a move. Awareness helps to free us to deal directly with problems and challenging situations.

The Level of Psychological Stress

Although *stress* is a household word these days, its usage came into vogue in the United States only at the end of World War II. During the war, health personnel noticed that some military men could not adapt to their duties. In concerned response, Grinker and Spiegel wrote *Men Under Stress*, and their book established the usage of this term.

Long before it was labeled, however, people have felt "stress." We experience psychological stress when we face an event we find threatening and with which we fear we cannot cope.[1] There are two kinds of stress. Chronic stress is a pervasive, long-lasting anxiety that persists through time and is the "typical" response of the individual. Acute stress is severe but temporary anxiety, arising in response to a life-changing event (such as a move).[2] Some people experience chronic stress daily, and any added pressure puts them on an emotional overload. Others meet every day problems without strain and can handle acute stress when it comes. Most of us fall somewhere in between.

Thomas Holmes and Richard Rahe were among the first researchers to score the effect of particular life stress events.[3] They asked over five thousand people questions such as, "How much distress would you feel if you were fired?" For each of forty-three such "events," they coded and averaged respondents' scores in terms of Life Changing Units (1-100 LCUs). These ranged from high stress (100 LCUs) for death of a spouse to low (11 LCUs) for minor violations of the law. Sometimes a positive event, such as outstanding personal achievements (28 LCUs), received a higher rating than a negative event, such as troubles with the boss (23 LCUs). Therefore, even celebrations can create strain.

According to Holmes and Rahe, people who accumulate too many LCUs in a short period of time may be in danger of a serious crisis. That is why those who face several recent pressures may want to avoid adding a move to their load. A crisis is more likely for those who already live with chronic stress and is less likely for those who handle acute stress well.

The life-event changes that are most apt to trigger a crisis are those that are unusual, unexpected, undesired, or uncontrollable, and that require a great deal of change in your daily routine.[4] These are common characteristics of some moves and help explain why certain moves are more difficult than others.

Evaluating a Situation and Your Ability to Cope

Two major factors that affect the amount of psychological stress you feel in a particular situation are (1) how you evaluate the situation and (2) your ability to deal with it.

In the first century A.D. the philosopher Epictetus wrote: "I am upset not by events, but by the way I view them." This statement has been quoted for centuries because it applies to many human situations. In other words, we tend to create our own reality by our attitude. If you see a party as dull, you will probably have a boring evening. If you define a new coworker as congenial, you are not likely to be disappointed. Similarly, your attitude toward a move can have a profound influence on whether it proves to be stressful or satisfying.

Of course, relocation is far more complex and harder to evaluate than a party. You take measure not only of the situation (what is at stake), but also of your competency to handle it. Stress begins when you face the possibility of a move and ends with adjustment to your new location. During the process of the move, your focus will shift from the situation (understanding the facts and implications of the move) to yourself (judging how well you are coping with the move). Your evaluation of the situation and of your coping ability takes place at three points in time: before you decide to move; after you decide; and throughout the relocation process (as there is evidence that your earlier projections were right or wrong). Lazarus' writings on appraisal are helpful here.[5]

Deciding to Move

The first task when faced with the possibility of a move is to look at the facts of the situation as you see them. "What is at stake?" "How beneficial will the move be to me and to those whom I love?" "How difficult will the move be?" "Is there potential harm to any of us in moving?" This harm might be current or anticipated; having to make a decision creates immediate stress and might also uncover seriously discrepant goals in your family. The anticipation of losses—of special friends and of a congenial community—adds to the anxiety.

Moving is always a gain-loss situation. You give up something of value in order to gain something else of value. Every member of a family wins and loses in relocation, but, as we point out in chapter 2, rewards and costs are seldom evenly distributed.

Unless a move is obviously beneficial, the view that the move is a challenge rather than a problem tips the scale in the direction of leaving, as does a favorable assessment of your coping ability. The outcome is affected as well as the decision. Viewing the move as a challenge at this time, as an opportunity for growth, offers the possibility of a positive outcome.

While your evaluating the situation in advance is important to understanding the psychological stress you will experience, so also is evaluating your ability to cope with the move. Confidence that you can handle it successfully is not a guarantee that you will, but the conviction that you cannot cope will seriously undermine your chances. Some of our respondents were overly optimistic and then were disappointed with themselves for having difficulty with a move. It is important to remember that by working through such an experience, we grow and gain strength to deal with other life events. Each new success gives greater confidence and increases our ability to cope.

After Deciding to Go

The choice has been made. The move is on. However, in choosing to move, you lose the option to stay, and you may feel torn. If you are like other movers who feel this internal tension, you may find yourself gathering evidence that you made the right choice. For example, if you are moving to Texas, you ignore acquaintances who tell you that in the summer you can bake a cake on any window ledge, and you treasure friends who talk of fresh air and wide open spaces. Looking at the positive side and gathering information affirms your decision.

However, there is an important difference between affirming a decision and denying your feelings of sadness. Denial is the refusal to acknowledge and deal with feelings of pain and conflict; it is an overestimation of your ability to cope. Denial is most common when neither choice is a happy one. For example, you dread a particular move, but refusing to go would threaten your marriage. A Pollyanna attitude can get you through the move, but you will eventually have to deal with feelings you have covered over.

> Over-optimism was my defense against incredible feelings of loss that I couldn't face at the time. I've had to deal with all of them in the two and a half years since we moved. If I had it to do over, I'd try to be more honest with myself from the start.

Time and energy are at a premium and are usually invested in moving on, rather than in letting go. One of our respondents indicated that probably no one can move without some denial. But the question is, how much?

Part of the disillusionment after a move may come from an assumption many of us make: A move will automatically create a fresh start, clearing up underlying family or individual problems. On the contrary, unfinished business only adds to the burdens of adjustment, and the resolution of such problems should be, at the very least, underway in advance. The move is not the time to sweep everything under the rug. Since heightened expectations, such as denial, make moving easier, but adjusting harder, feeling positive while facing reality is a fine line to walk.

During and After the Move

As you try to cope with a life event, you constantly shift your judgment about it. Appraisal that takes place at a later time is called reevaluation.

When you move, during the whole process and even after settling in has begun, you take inventory of how well the move is actually working out and of how well you are handling it. By now you have more information about your new setting and more awareness of how you have handled the change than you did previously. Any shift from your earlier judgments may be in a positive or negative direction.

Some reevaluations are especially jarring. A family man initiated a major move, only to realize three months later that not only were his four children and his wife miserable, but his new job was disappointing as well. He swallowed his pride by admitting to having made a poor decision. Several months later, back in their old community again, the family van unburdened itself of six happy people.

We found that advance expectations had a definite influence on reevaluation. Movers' expectations of the new location were apt to be lower and more realistic *before* a decision was made; afterward over-optimism inflated hopes and made reevaluation disillusioning. Overly high expectations—both of the new location and, as mentioned above, of our ability to handle the change—can create a disappointing ending. This is true even of those who are eager to move. Therefore, it is important to keep your expectations within realistic bounds.

For those of you who are realistic about the situation and your coping abilities and who consistently look at moving and settling in as a challenge rather than a threat, the move will usually be a positive experience. Good coping strategies are further insurance toward a successful outcome.

Adaptation and Coping Strategies

> To be healthy you have to adjust. I'm really good at problem solving. So when I am blue, I know what I have to do and how to get out of it. When my husband transferred, I said to myself, "If I want this to work, it will!"

"Adaptation" is "adjustment to reality."[6] It reduces stress and helps to maintain our inner balance. It is a powerful and natural response to stress that can be activated even before birth, as when an unborn child changes position in response to pressure on its mother's abdomen. Thus the natural (and almost automatic) ability to adapt begins early and continues throughout life. It is enhanced—in threatening situations—by the more complex, deliberate, and learned ability to cope.

Coping Mechanisms

When problems affect your welfare and tax your usual ways of adapting, you mobilize your coping mechanisms.[7] The verb *to cope* is an optimistic one. It means to struggle or to contend, with some degree of success. It implies challenge; you are equal to the problem you confront. The higher the stress level, the more demand is placed on your coping system.

Coping mechanisms may be directed *outward* toward the environment—making definite plans toward finding a job or structuring where you live—or *inward* toward the self—mobilizing inner resources through prayer or meditation. The coping mechanisms that you choose may or may not better the situation. For example, using "tension reduction" by indulging in excessive drinking will only create more problems. As the process of the move unfolds and as your evaluation of it shifts, different coping mechanisms may be activated and new ones developed.

Early in the process, many of us use familiar ways of coping in an effort to restore equilibrium. If that is not successful, trial and error follow. "The fact that I was not doing well sent me into a panic. I tried a little bit of everything to cope, thrashing around trying to find my center."

As further tension and threat build, the "make or break" phase is entered. Goals are changed; the problem is reinterpreted; or some element of hope is salvaged—anything to avoid feeling out of control. If even these last-ditch attempts fail, a crisis ensues, and we may want to seek professional help.

Fortunately, most of us manage to find adequate coping mechanisms before we reach this crisis point. Gradually, we learn more and better ways of adjusting to events, especially as we face and overcome difficult challenges. This personal growth is an important outcome of successfully handling life-changing events. When we can look back on highly stressful situations that we have mastered, we seldom want to change the past. We are who we are, stronger and wiser, because of these.

Specific Coping Mechanisms

To help identify specific coping mechanisms, Susan Folkman joined forces with Richard Lazarus in developing a Ways of Coping checklist.[8] It is used to learn how a person handles one particularly stressful event, rather than showing an overall coping style.

These authors divided sixty-six possibilities for coping into eight categories. We follow each category with an example of how the coping mechanisms may be used.

—Confrontive: I tried to get the person responsible to change his or her mind.

—Distancing: I made light of the situation; refused to get too serious about it.

—Self-controlling: I tried to keep my feelings to myself.

—Seeking Social Support: I talked to somebody about how I was feeling.

—Accepting Responsibility: I criticized and lectured myself.

—Escape/Avoidance: I wished the situation would go away or somehow be over.

—"Planful" Problem Solving: I knew what had to be done, so I doubled my efforts to make things work.

—Positive Reappraisal: I came out of the situation better than when I went in.*

*Adapted from Susan Folkman and Richard Lazarus, "The Ways of Coping Scales." Copyright © 1985 by the American Psychological Association. Reprinted by permission of the publisher and author.

In reading this list, perhaps you can have a better understanding of the way you have coped with a specific move. You probably leaned heavily on certain kinds of coping mechanisms. You may also have used other coping mechanisms. If some of them proved not to work for you, do not be discouraged. There are many other possibilities for you to try.

Adaptive and Maladaptive Ways of Coping

Many authorities agree on what are the most effective and least effective coping mechanisms for dealing with stress. These are listed below, starting with the least effective. Look at them and then look at the coping mechanisms that can work best for you. We have added illustrative quotations to each. You will note that the least effective mechanisms are passive in comparison to the most effective mechanisms. The latter involve an active pursuit of a happy ending to the potentially threatening event.

1. Distancing from the situation. "I went through the motions of moving, trying not to think of the changes ahead of me." When we use a lot of distancing, we have a head-in-the-sand outlook. We may be looking for rescue or perhaps we feel that the situation is just too difficult to face.

2. Escape/Avoidance. "I day-dreamed a lot about what my friends were doing and how it would be to be with them. I also put on ten pounds in the move!" Wishful thinking and denial are popular (and unhappy) choices.

3. Taking responsibility (or self-blame) "What was the matter with me? I'd known women who were unpacked and organized about a week after relocating. Yet, here I was—on the anniversary of our move—with *still* a dozen boxes unopened." Blaming yourself is a greased shute into depression, and it is hard to get out of that hole.

Now for eleven effective coping mechanisms.

1. Seeking social support. "We had a few old friends come out to visit, and we splurged on phone calls to get over the hump. It was also really important to join groups and make new friends as soon as possible." A passive role does not pay. Allow yourself to indulge in calling or writing old friends. You need them now. Also, reach out and get to know people. One woman we interviewed kept a file on new acquaintances. "It's easy to get them mixed up when you are meeting them for the first time."

2. *Problem solving.* "My way of coping? To make a plan for action and then follow it. For me it's therapeutic. If I didn't, I know I'd be a lot more depressed." When you complete a task, be sure to congratulate and reward yourself.

3. *Focusing on the positive* (a "Positive Reevaluation" technique). "I grew and learned from going to college. It was scary at times, but I focused on the good things that were happening to me." We are not suggesting that you deny your feelings. It is important for you to accept them and to sort out what you are experiencing. Such exploration gives you the opportunity to deal with the feelings. However, do not lose track of the positives.

4. *Exercising.* "I joined a recreation club and worked out as often as I could. As I looked better, I felt a lot better about myself." Exercise releases tension effectively, and the results of the exercise are more energy and a well-tuned body.

5. *Eating and sleeping well.* "A daily nap and regular balanced meals go a long way in warding off stress. When I was not well rested, I felt much worse." Lack of sleep can start as a symptom and become a massive problem. Be sure to get the rest you need and do not short-change yourself on good eating habits.

6. *Relying on your faith.* "When our baby died two days after reaching town, we needed God's comfort so badly. I remember going to our neighbors' home and waiting for them to answer the doorbell. They looked at our faces and welcomed us into their embrace and allowed us to weep with them as they sat near. So God provides for us in the present . . . and also promises us comfort for the future." Many of the persons with whom we talked spoke of deepened faith through the experience of struggle. Prayer, Bible reading, and church support are all important at times of stress and for continued functioning after the crisis is over.

7. *Understanding.* "Recognizing your roots helps maintain them and loosen them. When you realize just what you miss most, you are well on your way to replacing it in your life."[9] As mentioned in chapter 1, moving disrupts your basic meanings. If you take the time to search within, you can understand what is most important in your life and move on.

8. *Keeping a sense of humor.* Laughing at things that are strange quirks of fate can go a long way toward lightening any load. One woman's description of how to handle the move is, "Become ill and let your husband do it!" She said this jokingly, but, actually, she had done just that. She and her husband had gone out to dinner after their van had unloaded chaos into their new home. Food poisoning had put her to bed for four days—a hard way to get out of work!

9. *Keeping an open mind.* "Withholding judgment on your new home until at least two or three years have gone by will help. You *can* find things to enjoy, and people whom you may not have pictured as being potentially good friends may turn out to be such." Sometimes it takes a long time to settle in. Many who have found a particular move traumatic have ended up loving the new location. Give it and the people there a chance.

10. *Going with the flow.* An interviewee advised, "Hold all things loosely. Your life does not consist of your possesions . . . or your house."

11. *Communicating with others involved in the move.* "Mostly, I just let myself have the feelings. I talk them out and then take one day at a time." We have stressed this one over and over again. From the first discussion of the possibility of the move to the final settling in process (and beyond), this coping mechanism is terribly important. Sometimes we avoid communicating with others involved in the move because of not wanting to bother them, being overly preoccupied, feeling that the other person will not understand or will be upset by what we say, or viewing expressions of such feelings as a weakness. Do not let yourselves get caught up in these rationalizations.

Of course, no one uses the best coping mechanisms all the time. Do not fault yourselves if sometimes your ways of coping do not make sense to others. Also, please note that even a bad start can be corrected after the move with support from others and with improved coping mechanisms. It is important for you not to lose hope. Hope has been defined as "the sense of possibility . . . the sense of a way out and a destiny that goes somewhere, even if not to the specific place one had in mind."[10] Although you may not get exactly what you want, there is a direction and flow to the process through which you are going. A person's capacity to hope in the midst of a stressful situation can have a powerful influence on the outcome.

Notes

1. Susan Folkman and Richard Lazarus, "An Analysis of Coping in a Middle-Aged Community Sample." *Journal of Health and Social Behavior* 21 (September 1980):223.

2. Blair Wheaton, "Stress, Personal Coping Resources, and Psychiatric Symptoms." *Journal of Health and Social Behavior* 24 (September 1983):209.

3. Thomas Holmes and Richyard Rahe, "The Social Readjustment Rating Scale." *Journal of Psychosomatic Research* 11 (1967):213-18.

4. Joseph Zubin, "Discussion, Part IV, and Overview." In *Stress and Mental Disorder*, ed. James Barrett (New York: Raven Press, 1979), p. 284.

5. Richard Lazarus, *Psychological Stress and the Coping Process* (New York: McGraw-Hill, 1966), pp. 25ff.

6. Heinz Hartmann, *Ego Psychology and the Problem of Adaptation* (New York: International Universities Press, 1958; originally published in German in 1937), p. 3.

7. Richard Lazarus, James Averill, and E. Opton, "The Psychology of Coping: Issues of Research and Assessment." In *Coping and Adaptation*, eds. George Coelho, David Hamburg, and John Adams (New York: Basic Books, 1974), p. 250.

8. Susan Folkman and Richard Lazarus, "The Ways of Coping Scales," Stress and Coping Project, Department of Psychology, University of California, Berkeley, Calif. (1985).

9. Cynthia Van Hazinga, "Relief for the Uprooted." *Changing Homes.* 4 (Spring 1987):60.

10. Roy Fairchild, *Finding Hope Again* (New York: Harper, 1980), p. 51.

It's Your Move

> I remember the day it all turned around for me. I had been grieving for weeks. One morning I took out a piece of paper and made a list of short- and long-term goals. I followed this with a plan to implement these goals. From that day on, my spirits rose. I had taken charge of my life.

We have written this book for and about people who move. As we stated in the introduction, we had certain goals in mind for you, the reader: (1) We wanted to affirm your reactions and experiences, whether you are in the process of moving, have recently completed a move, or recall a difficult move from the past. (2) Our intent was to provide you with proven ways of coping and practical suggestions for relocation—insight into better ways of handling any future moves.

In the epilogue, we challenge you to take charge of your move, whether it is joyous or painful. We want you to make it an opportunity for personal growth.

Going through a move is a transitional experience and each transition has an ending, an interim period, and a new beginning.[1] These are not clearly delineated times. Rather, we move back and forth trying to find our former balance or to create a new one after the disruption of change. This flow occurs whether the transition is a maturational one having to do with physical and psychological growth; a family transition, such as any of us goes through with family life stages from marriage to the final separation of death or divorce; or the transitional experience of a life-changing event, such as moving. For this reason, much of what we wrote in the chapter on coping can also be helpful to you in other transitions.

The *endings* that any of us experiences with moving have to do with letting go of the previous home, environment, and, sometimes, cultural setting. Depending on earlier separations and on the depth of the bonding to the previous home, this may or may not be a difficult time for you. There will almost certainly be some grieving, since grief is a normal and important part of the process of letting go.[2] Leaving one's culture of origin, which "tugs at the very roots of identity," is particularly traumatic.[3]

The *interim* period is characterized by confusion while we settle into the new place. Often the feelings of sadness continue, and there is a sense of having a foot in two locations at the same time—your previous home and your new one. The tasks of this transition are: unpacking and beginning to feel a sense of belonging, understanding the "rules" of the new community, finding out where to get the best buys, locating doctors, and the many other things you have to do to be able to call a new place "home." If unemployed, you begin the process of a job search. You need to know that relocation, although common and to some extent satisfying, is disruptive. Your emotional reactions are normal and deserve expression. The woman quoted at the beginning of this chapter was in the interim period. She allowed herself time for sadness, but when she was ready, she took hold of the situation and found a way to move forward.

By making a list of goals, which proved to be her step toward change, she entered the phase of *new beginnings*. In this phase, you make friends, learn the ropes of the new position, join a church or synagogue, and find groups of people with whom you are compatible. Finally you achieve your former state of balance and invest yourself in the new life experience.

The woman quoted below describes the overall process.

When I knew we were to be transferred, I hoped we would go South, near my folks, not to the Dakotas or Wisconsin [other alternatives]. When my husband came home and said "Milwaukee," my heart sank. I felt sad about both leaving where we were and not being able to go where I wanted to. After we moved, I found another relocated wife next door, and we complained and moped and overate together. She started attending Weight Watchers and buying doughnuts on the way home. "No way!" I said and decided to find out what my new environment had to offer. I piled the kids in the van, and on the first day we found a number of nearby fishing lakes. "Just like down South," I said. So fishing was our recreation all summer. Then I helped my doughnut friend get into aerobic dance.

Accepting the Challenge of Change

As indicated above, the change experienced in a move is always somewhat disruptive. We build comfort into our home and environment—rather like a bird moving around inside its nest until the contours are just right for its body. In addition, we also build into our living situation enough stimuli to keep us feeling alert and alive. Once we have found the right combination, we may not want to move. Among the men and women we interviewed, the greatest resistance to moving came from those who had finally created their "best of all possible worlds."

Moving, starting fresh in a new community, besides being a change, can also be greeted as a challenge. We encourage you to see it as such. A move is an opportunity to stretch and to grow as a person, a satisfaction known by many people on the move. Some of our interviewees credited themselves because the act of moving was a victory for them. Some celebrated major shifts in their lives—changes in career or marital status, for example—in addition to relocation. Still others accepted the challenge of change, not in moving, but in deciding not to go. They found new ways to grow within the stable setting of their current situation.

In an important way, the men, women, and children whom we interviewed are joint authors with us to explore this challenge from both a psychological and a practical standpoint. Their real-life examples of the ups and downs of relocation have made this book possible. Those we talked to also helped us accomplish the goals we held for you, our readers, which we mentioned at the beginning of this epilogue. Their stories, as we have told them, cannot reflect the depth of feeling or the height of emotion expressed by person after person.

We recall the pleasure of the majority of those we interviewed for whom moves have turned out to be positive after a certain period of adjustment. Career improvement, personal growth, new learning in adaptability and flexibility, marital growth, and family growth that resulted in a new sense of unity and purpose mark some of the dividends in the moves. There is excitement in going to a new location, broadening horizons, and finding that social and communication skills have improved.

As we come to the end of this book, we hope that you have gained not only a heightened awareness of the potential problems inherent in moving, but also an understanding of ways to meet these problems and to build in opportunities. May the information and practical instruments we have provided help you put your best efforts into making successful moves. Congratulations—it's *your* opportunity! It's *your* move!

Notes

1. William Bridges, *Transitions* (Menlo Park, Calif.: Addison Wesley, 1980), pp. 5 and 9.
2. Eric Klinger, "Consequences and Commitment to and Disengagement from Incentives." *Psychological Review* 82 (January 1975):1 ff.
3. Marshal H. Levy-Warren, "Moving to a New Culture: Cultural Identity, Loss and Mourning." In *Psychology and Separation and Loss,* eds. Jonathan Bloom-Feshbach, Sally Bloom-Feshbach, and Associates (San Francisco: Jossey-Bass, 1987), p. 301.

INDEX

Adaptation, 146-47
American Association of Retired Persons, 119
American Womens' Clubs, 113
The Army Wife (Shea), 101-2

Beethoven, Ludwig, 16
Bowlby, John, 19

Children, 35, 71-73, 76-78, 109, 114, 129-30
  adolescent, 74-76, 103, 109, 112, 137-38
  choosing a school for, 78-80
  coping with a move and, 75-76, 80-81
  divorce and, 95-96
  international moves and, 109, 114
  rewards for moving and, 81-82
  other issues and, 81
  young, 73-74, 131-33, 137-38
Clari, the Maid of Milan, 15
College and moving, 83-88
Commuter marriages, 60-63
Coping mechanisms, 75-76, 147-52
Coping with a move
  children and, 75-76, 80-81
  evaluating a situation and, 143-52
  singles and, 97-99
Corporations and moves, 26, 29-31, 48, 59-60, 67-69, 89-91, 104, 109-11, 116
Couples
  commuter marriages and, 60-63
  homemaker and career, 63-66
  men moving for their partners and, 29, 57-58, 91-92

multiple moves and, 66-67
resistance to moving and, 30, 67-69, 94, 109
working, 55-60, 104, 109, 117
Daldlianus, 16
Deciding to move
  authority with regard to, 31-32
  costs of, 25-26, 33-37, 72-73
  equity regarding, 42-43, 48-51, 57-58, 69-70
  personality and, 32-33
  questionnaire regarding, 40-51
  reasons for, 26-32, 64, 88-92, 94-96, 107
  rewards of, 37-40, 64, 81-82, 98-99, 155-56
  retirement and, 119-21
Divorce and single parents, 92-97

Empathy, importance of, 20, 69-70, 76-77
Employee Relocation Council, 29
Epictetus, 143

Folkman, Susan, 148

Gilligan, Carol, 64
Grief and loss, 20, 31, 36, 56, 64-69, 71-72, 81, 92-95, 114, 121, 145, 154
Grinker, Roy, 142

Holmes, Thomas, 142-43
Home
  affective quality of, 21-23
  feeling response to, 18-23